# 30-Day Anti-Inflammatory Meal Plan Cookbook

## Scrumptious Recipes To Fight Inflammatory Diseases & Restore Overall Health

MATT PYNE

ISBN-13:978-1718941212

ISBN-10:1718941218

DEDICATION

For Cindy,

Pleasant memories, always!

# TABLE OF CONTENTS

# INTRODUCTION

## Understanding Inflammation

Inflammation is a natural and immediate response to infection, irritation or injury. It is how our immune system responds to injury. If you scrape your knee, for instance, your body reacts immediately with pain and redness around that area. Your white blood cells, having received these signals, set off an immediate response to deal with the problem. These reactions make it impossible for the body to do further damage to the wound or injury while it heals. This type of inflammation is known as acute inflammation. It is a normal and healthy process that activates our immune system and destroys invading pathogens. Without inflammation, it will be impossible to be healed of injuries, infections, diseases and other illnesses. Acute inflammation is a good thing. It is a protective measure to remove harmful invaders in order for the body to repair and heal. It is localized and short-term as it disappears once healing has taken place.

Chronic inflammation is totally different. In this case, the inflammation occurs for long periods of time. This signifies that something has gone wrong with the immune process. Your body is in conflict because it is trying to heal and simultaneously destroy infection or dead tissue. As it strives to quash the original injury, the irritant keeps penetrating the body. This is a problem because if the immune system fails to work well, the affected person will be prone to a myriad of diseases that can affect every aspects of daily existence. This continuous and invisible inflammation has been associated with various diseases, cancer, arthritis and other grave illnesses.

Chronic inflammation can be caused by several factors such as exposure to toxins, personal genetics, poor nutrition, stress, a lack of exercise and dependence on medication. But, diet has been identified as one of its major causes. Inflammation is triggered by consuming lots of processed foods, junk foods, refined white sugar, artificial sweeteners, high-heat treated refined vegetable and seed oils, food additives, high-fructose corn syrup, alcohol, refined grains, soft drinks, preservatives, nitrates, pesticides, factory-farm raised animals and genetically modified foods. In fact, the typical American diet is packed with inflammatory foods, resulting in illnesses. Chronic inflammation is systemic; it affects the organs, digestive system and of course, the immune system.

Health Conditions Linked To Chronic Inflammation:

These include:

- Autoimmune diseases like rheumatoid arthritis, leaky gut and inflammatory bowel disease.
- High blood pressure and coronary heart disease such as atherosclerosis and heart attacks.
- Breakdown of the immune system, leading to degenerative diseases.
- Premature aging and chronic pain in the body such as migraine headaches, joint pain and Alzheimer's disease.
- Periodontitis, a condition where gums retreat away from the teeth.
- Certain cancers like gallbladder carcinoma.
- Hay fever (the allergic reaction to pollen) and asthma.
- Necrosis (destruction of the tissue) by the inflammatory cells.

In fact, chronic inflammation is linked with higher amounts of oxidative stress and many chronic diseases too many to be mentioned. To reduce chronic inflammation, you will have to remove or at least limit the foods that cause it, and increase the foods that reduce it.

The nutritional composition of your diet produces inflammatory and anti-inflammatory chemicals known as prostaglandins. Prostaglandins affect's your body's inflammatory response. For this reason, you should eat foods with very high omega-3 fatty acids and antioxidants as this helps your body to create more anti-inflammatory prostaglandins.

Also, eat foods that help to build a strong immune system. A strong immune system easily wards off diseases, illnesses and free radicals. Eat foods devoid of artificial or process ingredients. Go for high-fiber rather than refined grains, whole-foods rather than processed, food high in healthy fats and foods low in transfats as well as some anti-inflammatory spices. Once you improve your food and lifestyle choices, you can easily eliminate chronic inflammation from your body.

## Symptoms Of Inflammation

These include:

- Persistent irritating pain in the body ( Joint & muscle pain)
- Irritable Bowel Syndrome and Ulcers (diarrhea or constipation)
- Skin problems or red eyes
- Constant fatigue/loss of energy
- High blood pressure or blood sugar problems
- Aggravating allergies or asthma
- Joint stiffness & Loss of joint function
- General "flu"-like symptoms such as fever, chills, headaches and loss of appetite.

## Tests For Inflammation

To find out if you have chronic inflammation; ask your doctor to carry out any these 6 common inflammatory markers:

- High levels of Homocysteine
- Elevated Blood Glucose
- Elevated Ferritin in the blood

- Elevated HDL
- SED Rate
- Elevated High Sensitivity C-Reactive Protein (HS-CRP)
- Elevated Monocytes

If at least 2 of these tests show that you have signs of chronic inflammation, then you need to start making anti-inflammatory choices immediately. There is no time to waste; you are either pro-inflammatory or anti-inflammatory.

While it is easy to delay or postpone your choices because chronic inflammation is long- term, you should remember that pro-inflammatory choices add up eventually and will one day become the reason for that heart disease, Inflammatory Bowel Disease or even that cause of death!

# Pro-Inflammatory And Anti-Inflammatory Foods

As earlier stated, the foods we consume can either trigger or prevent chronic inflammatory conditions. Knowing the best foods that fight inflammation (anti- inflammatory foods) as well as the foods that worsen it (pro-inflammatory foods) will enable you plan your meals and watch what you eat. Whether you are on a Paleo, vegan or Mediterranean diet, you can manage inflammation and lead a healthy lifestyle.

## Pro- Inflammatory Foods

Pro- inflammatory foods lead to weight gain and premature aging. If you load your body with starchy, sugary and processed foods, the result will be an overweight body and a poor health.

## Pro- Inflammatory Foods Include:

- <u>Sugar</u>: candy, coffee drinks, soda, snack bars, baked sweets and more.

- <u>Highly Refined flours</u> such as white bread, crackers, flour tortillas, Pizza, pasta, bagels, and pretzels. (Limit your consumption of pasta to once in a week).

- <u>Refined Carbohydrates</u> such as white rice, processed cereals, chips and French fries.

- And <u>Refined Corn</u> and corn derivatives such as corn starch, corn oil and high-fructose corn syrup often used by food industry on account of their availability and cheap cost. All these highly refined foods digest very quickly, raising blood sugar and causing an increase in insulin. This leads to an inflammatory response in the body.

- <u>Seed Oils:</u> Seed oils like sunflower oil, canola oil, Soybean oil, safflower oil, corn oil, peanut oil, cottonseed oil and foods prepared with these oils such as margarine, tartar sauce, salad dressings, mayonnaise, and many packaged foods. These foods are highly processed and contain lots of unhealthy omega-6 fatty acids.

- <u>Fried Foods:</u> French fries, fish sticks, fried chicken, onion rings and anything that is fried.

- <u>Dairy:</u> such as butter, non-dairy coffee creamers, cheese and whole milk. Yoghurt may be taken, but moderately, because it contains probiotics that help to lessen inflammation. Other dairy products contain lots of lactose and casein that causes inflammation.

- Partially Hydrogenated Oils (Trans fats) usually found in margarine, French fries and many packaged foods. <u>These packaged foods</u> have had their shelf life prolonged with preservatives, artificial flavorings and, colorings, which trigger inflammation in the body.

- <u>Processed Meats:</u> hot dogs, sausage, bacon and jerky are some examples of processed meats that are high in saturated fats and also contain substantial levels of AGEs (advanced glycation end products). The processes of drying, smoking or pasteurizing these meats causes inflammatory compounds to form. They may also be injected with preservatives, and artificial flavors that weaken the immune system.

- <u>Grain-Fed Meat</u> like beef and pork may cause digestion troubles for people with sensitive stomachs. Grain-fed animals are often given antibiotics and hormones to keep them alive. Their meats and eggs will contain bacterial toxins that can trigger endotoxins in the blood. To be safe, go for grass-fed meats.

- Artificial Sweeteners: such as Splenda, and any no-calorie "Diet" soft drinks.

- Alcohol: avoid all alcohol beverages as it cause inflammation in the liver and other areas such as tissues, guts and blood vessels.

- Artificial Additives: such as ice creams and candies, contain artificial addictives like coloring and flavoring. Your body cannot digest these addictives so it fights them. This is what results in inflammation.

- Nuts And Seeds: such as peanuts and peanut butter. Peanuts are very common food allergens with naturally occurring molds on them. While you may not have anaphylactic reaction to peanuts, you body could still see them as unfamiliar invaders and cause an inflammatory response.

- Spices And Condiments : ketchup, BBQ sauce, chutney with added sugar, soy sauce and salad dressings.

- Soy milk, and any product made from soy.

- Starch: Wheat, oats (including oatmeal), barley, rye, spelt, kamut, and any gluten product.

**Top Anti-Inflammatory Foods**

Anti- inflammatory foods are generally a healthy low fat diet. They include:

Raw, Organic Green Leafy Vegetables – these include kale, baby lettuce, spinach, arugula, butter lettuce, collard greens, watercress, green oak leaf lettuce, chicory, mustard greens, mache, red oak leaf lettuce, turnip greens, Swiss chard and romaine lettuce. Greens Leafy vegetables are nutrient-packed and high in minerals, vitamins, fiber, antioxidants, phytochemicals, chlorophyll, sulfur, enzymes and silicon which all fight inflammation.

Organic, Cruciferous Vegetables – these include cabbage, arugula, kale, broccoli, Brussel sprouts, watercress. bok choy, collard greens, rutabaga, cauliflower, mustard greens, kohlrabi, radishes, turnips and turnip greens. These are nutrient dense vegetables that are also high in vitamin C, minerals, fiber, beta carotene, phytochemicals, chlorophyll, enzymes and glucosinolates. Organic cruciferous vegetables protect the body from inflammation, remove toxins and prevent cancer.

Organic, raw fruits – these include all blackberries, raspberries, strawberries, blueberries, and black grapes. They contain flavonoids which are powerful antioxidants as well as phytochemicals and which help fight inflammation, prevent premature aging and protect the body against damage caused by free radicals.

Other fruits in this category include apples, avocado, cherries, cantaloupe, guava, figs, kiwi, kumquats, limes, lemons, mangoes, oranges, pears, papaya, tomatoes and pineapples. They all help to fight inflammation in the body.

Raw Organic Seeds And Nuts – Raw seeds and nuts such as chia seeds, hemp seeds, flax seeds and walnuts are excellent source of omega 3 fatty acids, which are powerful inflammation fighters. They also provide the body with protein, B vitamins, minerals, vitamin E, enzymes, fiber, potassium, selenium, magnesium, zinc, iron and copper.

Organic Bell Peppers (Red, Yellow & Orange,) – Organic bell peppers are loaded with flavonoids, antioxidants, fiber, phytochemicals, silicon, vitamin E, vitamin C, vitamin A and lycopene, that protect the body against inflammation and promote vascular health.

Wild Seafood – Wild seafood contains the essential omega 3 fatty acids DHA and EPA which produce anti-inflammatory compounds known as eicosanoids in our body. It is also an excellent source of protein. Salmon, anchovies, sardines, herring, mackerel, black cod and halibut are good examples. Do not fry but poach, bake, steam or broil.

Herbs– basil, dill, cilantro, sage, mint, parsley, oregano, rosemary and thyme are top herbs which fight inflammation. Rosemary is very high in rosmarinic acid, an antioxidant that lowers inflammation responses in the body.

Allium family – The allium family includes onion, garlic, leeks, chives, shallots and scallions. They are rich in vitamins, minerals, flavonoids (quercetin), antioxidants, fiber and enzymes. Their high sulphur content helps to fight against premature aging. The allium family also makes it possible for the liver to get rid of toxins and carcinogens that cause chronic inflammation.

Spices– spices such as turmeric, cloves, nutmeg, cinnamon, ginger and chili peppers help to fight inflammation. Ginger contains a compound called gingerol a compound which is renowned for its inflammatory inhibitory properties.

Olives And Olive Oil – Olives are rich in omega 3 and oleic fatty acids, vitamin E, vitamin A, calcium and protein. Olives also contain polyphenols, a potent antioxidant and phytochemical that protects the heart. Additionally, the body converts the healthy monounsaturated fat which is found in olives to anti-inflammatory agents.

Starch: Brown rice, millet, amaranth, quinoa, sweet potatoes, tapioca, buckwheat.

Bread/Cereal: rice products, buckwheat, tapioca, amaranth, arrowroot, quinoa

Tea: Kombucha tea, green tea and herbal teas which are not only packed with anti-inflammatory properties but can be made in many different delicious ways. Green, white, and oolong tea are packed with antioxidants, inflammation- limiting compounds.

Sweeteners: Fruit sweeteners, Brown rice syrup, yacon syrup, blackstrap molasses, coconut crystals, stevia, coconut palm sugar.

Grass-Fed Meat Or Wild Game: lean meat, skinless chicken and omega-3 eggs and fish

<u>Dark Chocolate/ Raw Cacao</u> – these two contain top antioxidants, flavonoids, polyphenols, fiber and magnesium that protect the body against accelerated aging and inflammation. The dark chocolate must have at least 60 percent to 70 of cacao for maximum health benefits.

# Cooking Methods To Reduce Inflammation

Besides choosing the right foods, you must also choose the right cooking methods to prepare these foods. If you cook the wrong way, you will end up undoing a lot of the good in your healthy foods and your anti-inflammatory diet.

Below are a few cooking methods tips:

**<u>Steaming</u>**: —

Steamed foods are prepared in steaming baskets or special bamboos that can be placed over boiling water. Proper steaming preserves the nutrients, crispness and color of vegetables. Simply create your own steamer with a covered pot and slotted insert. Chop vegetables into small chunks to enable them steam more quickly and evenly. Be careful not to overcook your vegetables, even fish or seafood. Foods with herbs like sage and rosemary should be marinated before steaming. Reheat quinoa and rice by steaming. Also, add spices like turmeric and ginger to foods while steaming to infuse the flavor into the food.

**<u>Baking</u>:** Put your fish or chicken in the center of a baking dish, preferably glass or ceramic. Leave room around the sides of the dish to enable hot air to circulate. Set vegetables on the bottom, under meat or fish, to add moisture and enhance flavor. Cover the dish so the food can cook with steam while preserving its natural juices.

**<u>Stir-Frying</u>:** This method involves stirring and tossing foods quickly in a small amount of oil at high temperatures to enable the food absorb the oil. Quick cooking helps to retain vitamins and minerals. Vegetables specifically retain their beneficial nutrients.

Different foods require different cook time. Foods that take the longest to cook should be added first to the wok or pan.

For instance; onions, sweet potatoes, carrots, winter squash, leeks and celery should go in first.

Green beans, cabbage, cauliflower, zucchini and broccoli should go in next and lastly greens, snow peas, green peas and bean sprouts.


## Blanching / Parboil

This method involves boiling foods very quickly. Bring water to a boil, drop in the chopped and washed veggies quickly for a minute or less, remove from the heat, strain and rinse under cold water. This method removes the raw edge off vegetables to be enjoyed as salads and crudités.


**Poaching:** This gentle cooking method involves submerging food fully or partially in barely simmering liquid. It requires no extra fats like oil. Bring water or stock to a boil, add your veggies, meat or seafood; lower the heat and simmer until done. Keep the poaching liquid to use it as the base of a soup.

**Note:** Avoid microwaving.

# 30- DAY ANTI-INFLAMMATION MEAL PLAN RECIPES

## Breakfast Ideas

*Ideas for a hearty breakfast to lower inflammation include*

- *homemade smoothies*
- *some organic egg dishes*
- *pitted and fitted avocado with tuna*
- *gluten- and wheat-free toast like rice bread*
- *breakfast sausages without addictives*
- *Gluten-free packaged pancake mix with bananas or berries and sweetened with coconut crystals or yacon syrup.*

**Snacks Ideas**

*Fruits and nuts are excellent on-the-go snacks, packed with nutrients and filled with omega-3 fatty acids which are found in most nuts. The simplest natural snack is a handful of fresh vegetables or fruit like some snow peas and crispy apple. You could also, stuff a large portobello mushroom with kale, assemble an avocado dip or enjoy a handful of dates.*

*Other ideas for snacking include:*

- *Celery ribs filled with almond butter*
- *Crackers or gluten-free bread with 2 tablespoons of nut butter*
- *Brown rice, avocado and mango*
- *Raw veggies with hummus*
- *1 medium grapefruit and a hard-boiled egg*
- *Sardines packed in extra virgin olive oil with rice crackers*
- *1/2 cup of unsweetened applesauce and almonds*
- *Organic cold roasted chicken dipped in mustard*
- *1/2 cup of blueberries, especially for nighttime*
- *Dark chocolates*
- *Make popsicles by blending together ripe mangos, ground turmeric, a fresh ginger piece, cashews, maple syrup, and water. pour into popsicle molds and freeze.*
- *Yogurt with blueberries and almonds.*

.

# DAY 1

## Breakfast

### Strawberry Pecan Oatmeal

Prep Time: 2 minutes

Cook Time: 0 minutes

Serves: 2

**Ingredients**

2 cups of cooked oatmeal (not instant)

1 cup strawberries, hulled& chopped

2 tablespoons pecans, crushed

2 cups 1% milk

1/4 cup of organic real maple syrup

**Directions**

1. Add the strawberries to the oatmeal and stir well.

2. Pour into bowls and top with the maple syrup and nuts. Serve with the milk.

# Lunch

## Beet Salad

*Beets have great antioxidant properties, which gives them their brilliant red color. They are also loaded with vitamin C as well as plant pigments called fiber and betalains, which help to fight inflammation and lower the risk of cancer and heart disease. Beets also contain butane, which makes it easier to digest foods.*

Prep Time: 10 minutes

Cook Time: 0 minutes

Serves: 4

### Ingredients:

1 beet, coarsely grated

1 carrot, coarsely grated

1 large apple, diced

2 tablespoons of almonds, chopped

2 tablespoons of lemon juice

2 tablespoons of pumpkin seed oil

4 cups mixed greens

2 garlic cloves, minced, optional

2 tablespoons of fresh chopped dill or parsley, optional

1/4 teaspoon gray sea salt or pink rock salt, optional

### Directions:

1. Add together all the ingredients, except the mixed greens, in a large bowl and toss well.

2. Add in the optional ingredients if using.

3. Place greens onto plates and top with beet and the mixture.

# Dinner

## Chicken Fajita Stuffed Peppers

Prep Time: 75 minutes

Cook Time: 25 minutes

Serves: 4

**<u>Ingredients:</u>**

14 oz boneless skinless chicken breasts, cut into strips

1 cup black beans, rinsed and drained

2 tablespoons fresh cilantro, chopped

1 teaspoon cumin seed

1/2 teaspoon oregano

1 teaspoon chili powder

1/2 teaspoon garlic powder

1 lime - zested & juiced

1/4 teaspoon red pepper flakes

1/2 avocado, diced

3 teaspoons olive oil, divided

1/4 cup fresh cilantro, chopped

1/4 cup 0%-Fat Greek yogurt

2 tablespoons fresh squeezed lime juice

16 cherry tomatoes, sliced

1 large onion, sliced

4 whole bell peppers

4 nectarines

## Directions

1. Combine the red pepper flakes, cumin seeds, garlic powder, chili powder, oregano in a bowl, mixing well. Alternatively grind in a coffee grinder.

2. Add lime juice, lime zest, and 1 teaspoon of olive oil. Pour mixture over chicken, cover and chill overnight or at least for 1hour.

3. In a deep bowl, add yogurt, avocado and lime juice blended with a food processor. Add 1/4 cup of cilantro, stir and cover with plastic wrap and then set aside.

4. Heat the olive oil that's left in a skillet over medium-high heat. Add the onions and sauté 10 minutes, remove and set aside.

5. Add the chicken to the same pan and sauté about 8 minutes until cooked through. Add the cooked onions, tomatoes and beans, stir and cook 1 minute until well mixed.

6. Remove from heat. Place pepper on a plate, fill with 1 cup chicken and veggies. Top with 1 tablespoon of the cilantro/ avocado mixture.

# Snacks

## Snack Mix Time

Prep Time: 5 minutes

Cook Time: 5 minutes

Serves: 6

### Ingredients

6 tablespoons organic golden raisins

¼ cup raw, unsalted cashews

¼ cup raw, unsalted whole almonds

¼ cup raw, unsalted pecan halves

6 tablespoons dried organic cranberries

¼ cup raw, unsalted walnuts pieces

¼ cup hulled raw, unsalted sunflower seeds

### Directions

1. Preheat oven to 400 degrees F. Combine the sunflower seeds, cashews, almonds, pecans and walnuts on a baking sheet.

2. Bake for 5 minutes then cool slightly. Add the raisin and dried cranberries, mixing well.

3. Store covered in air tight glass bowls.

# DAY 2

## Breakfast

### Avocado, Cheese& Anchovies On Toast

Prep Time: 5 minutes

Cook Time: minutes

Serves: 1

**Ingredients**

1 slice of toasted bread, gluten-free

½ avocado

Goat cheese

Anchovies

**Directions**

1. Top the toasted gluten-free bread with cheese and avocado, spreading nicely.

2. Enjoy with a glass of orange juice.

# Lunch

## Healthy Slaw Recipe

*There are lots of heart-healthy properties in this recipe with its antioxidant-rich broccoli, lemon, onions and cabbage.*

Prep Time: 1 hour 5 minutes

Cook Time: 0 minute

Serves: 6

### Ingredients

3 cups raw broccoli slaw, shredded

1 head shredded cabbage

2 tablespoons mayonnaise

1/4 cup non-fat Greek yogurt

1 tablespoon lemon juice, freshly squeezed

1 tablespoon fresh lemon zest

2 teaspoons honey

1 tablespoon apple cider vinegar

1/2 teaspoon Home Seasoning (recipe follows)

1 green onion, chopped

1/8 cup fresh parsley leaves, chopped

For the Home Seasoning

Combine1/4 cup of pepper, 1 cup salt &1/4 cup garlic powder and then mix well to combine.

### Directions

1. In a large bowl, add the cabbage and broccoli slaw together.

2. Whisk together 1/2 teaspoon of the House Seasoning, the mayonnaise, honey yogurt, vinegar, lemon juice and zest. Pour dressing over slaw and toss to coat.

3. Add the green onions and parsley and toss once more.

4. Cover with plastic wrap, place in the refrigerator for 1 hour. Serve and enjoy.

*Blueberry And Baby Green Salad*

# Dinner

## Mediterranean -Flavored Tofu With Herbs & Sautéed Spinach

*This balsamic marinated tofu cooks to a beautiful brown color with crispy edges. Give some time to press and also drain the tofu before cooking.*

Prep Time: 2 hours

Cook Time: 5 minutes

Serves: 4

### Ingredients

For The Tofu

1 (14-oz.) package extra-firm tofu, cut into 2

4 tablespoons of extra-virgin olive oil

1 teaspoon of minced rosemary

1 teaspoon of minced thyme

¼ teaspoon of sea salt

2 tablespoons of balsamic vinegar

1 teaspoon of minced garlic

1 teaspoon of minced parsley

½ teaspoon of coarsely ground black pepper

### Directions

1. Slice each cut piece of tofu horizontally, in half, to make 4 slices.

2. Drain the tofu by placing the slices in one layer on a shallow tray and then placing paper towels on top and underneath the tofu. Next, place

another tray on top of the tofu and use a heavy skillet to weigh it down. Refrigerate 30-60 minutes.

3. Meanwhile, add together garlic, 2 tablespoons extra-virgin olive oil, rosemary, vinegar, thyme, parsley, salt and pepper.

4. After draining the tofu, discard the excess liquid and pat dry. Place the tofu in a dish and pour the balsamic marinade over it. Chill at least 30 minutes.

5. Heat the remaining extra-virgin olive oil in a skillet over medium-high heat. Cook the tofu for 2-3 minutes per side, until brown. Transfer to a plate. Serve topped with sautéed spinach with lemon and garlic.

## Snacks

### Nutty Berries

Serves: 1

### Ingredients

1 tablespoon slivered almonds

1/4 cup 0%-Fat Greek yogurt

1/3 cup of blueberries

### Directions

Combine all the ingredients in a bowl and enjoy.

# DAY 3

## Breakfast

## Ginger Carrot Turmeric Smoothie

*This anti-inflammatory smoothie with its immune-boosting properties can be enjoyed for breakfast*

Prep Time: 15 minutes

Cook Time: 0 minute

Serves: 2

### Ingredients

For The Carrot Juice

1 1/2 cups filtered water

2 cups carrots

For The Smoothie

1 large ripe banana, previously peeled, sliced &frozen

1 cup pineapple, frozen or fresh

1/2 tablespoon of fresh ginger, peeled

1/2 cup carrot juice

1/4 teaspoon ground turmeric

1 tablespoon of lemon juice

1 cup unsweetened almond milk

### Directions

1. To make the carrot juice, add the carrots and water to a blender and blend until pureed and smooth. If necessary, add more water.

2. Drape a dish towel over a mixing bowl and then pour over the juice. Lift the corners of the towel up and then start to twist and squeeze out the juice until the liquid is completely extracted. Save the pulp for smoothies, or carrot muffins. Store carrot juice in a mason jar.

3. Next, add the smoothie ingredients to the blender and blend until creamy and smooth. If necessary, add more almond milk or carrot juice.

4. Taste for flavors then add more pineapple or banana for sweetness; ginger for bite; turmeric for warmth, and lemon for acidity.

*Chia Smoothie*

# Lunch

## Sweet & Spicy Broccoli

Prep Time: 10 minutes

Cook Time: 15 minutes

Serves: 3

### Ingredients

3 cups fresh broccoli florets

1 tablespoon olive oil

1 teaspoon red pepper flakes

3 tablespoons grated parmesan cheese

1 teaspoon brown sugar, packed

Salt and black pepper

### Directions

1. Pour water into a large pan and bring to a boil. Fill a bowl with half water and half ice cubes. Put the broccoli into the boiled water for 1 to 2 minutes; remove and put into cold water to cool the broccoli.

2. Mix brown sugar and parmesan cheese together in a bowl. Place the cooled broccoli in a small bowl wrapped with paper towel, to help drain water.

3. Add oil to a wok or a large skillet and heat. Add broccoli, red pepper flakes, pepper and salt. Cook and stir for 3 to 4 minutes.

4. Remove from cooker; add parmesan mixture and mix well.

# Dinner

## Quinoa And Turkey Stuffed Peppers

Prep Time: 10 minutes

Cook Time: 35 minutes

Serves: 6

### Ingredients:

1 cup uncooked quinoa

3 red bell peppers cut in half , membranes and seeds out

1/2 teaspoon salt

1/2 lb. smoked turkey sausage, diced & cooked

1/2 cup chicken stock

1/4 cup extra-virgin olive oil

3 tablespoons pecans, toasted &chopped

2 tablespoons fresh parsley, chopped

2 teaspoons fresh rosemary, chopped

2 cups of water

### Directions

1. Combine the quinoa, water and salt in a saucepan, set heat to high and bring to a boil. Lower heat to low, cover and simmer 15 minutes.

2. Once the water is fully absorbed, uncover and set aside for 5 minutes. Add in the chicken stock, sausage, oil, parsley, pecans and rosemary, stirring well.

3. Cook the peppers in boiling water for 5 minutes, drain and fill with the quinoa mixture. Place stuffed peppers in a lightly greased baking dish and bake at 350°F for 15 minutes.

# Snacks

## Indian Curried Cashews

Prep Time: 10 minutes

Cook Time: 20 minutes

Serves: 8

### Ingredients

2 cups of raw &unsalted cashews

1 tsp Madras curry powder

2 teaspoon extra-virgin olive oil

½ teaspoon sea salt

½ tsp ground coriander

½ tsp ground fenugreek

½ tsp cumin, ground

½ tsp cinnamon, ground

½ tsp ground chile pepper

### Directions

1. Preheat oven to 300 degrees F. Toss together the cashews and extra-virgin olive oil on a baking sheet.

2. Combine the curry powder, ground chile pepper, coriander, salt, cumin, fenugreek and cinnamon in a small bowl. Sprinkle over the cashews then turn over to coat well.

3. Bake until fragrant and golden brown. Serve warm.

# DAY 4

## Breakfast

### Gluten-Free Morning Crepes
Prep Time: 10 minutes

Cook Time: 15 minutes

Yield: 6

**Ingredients**

1 cup gluten-free all purpose flour

1 teaspoon vanilla, gluten-free

2 eggs

1/2 cup water

1/2 cup nut milk

1/4 teaspoon salt

2 tablespoons coconut oil, melted

1-2 tablespoons agave nectar

1 tablespoon coconut oil, for pan

**Directions**

1. Melt 2 tablespoons of coconut oil in a small saucepan over low heat.

2. Whisk together the eggs, nut milk, vanilla, agave nectar, water and salt in a mixing bowl until combined. Add in the flour gradually and whisk well to combine.

3. Remove oil from heat; pour into batter while whisking slowly to combine. Mix until smooth.

4. Heat the coconut oil over medium high heat. Pour the batter onto the griddle, using about 1/3 cup for each crepe. Tilt and swirl the pan so that the batter coats the surface well.

5. Cook the crepe for 2 minutes. Once the bottom is light brown, flip with a spatula and cook the other side. Do this with the rest of the batter.

# Lunch

## Curried Waldorf Salad
*Dairy-free and nut-free, this traditional favorite will leave you craving for more!*

Prep Time: 10 minutes

Cook Time: 15 minutes

Serves: 2

### Ingredients:

¼ cup of chopped walnuts

1 large Gala apple, skin on, cored& diced

1 cup extra-firm tofu, drained & cut into 1-inch cubes

½ cup chopped celery

½ tablespoon of ground flaxseed

½ teaspoon grated fresh ginger

½ teaspoon curry powder

1 head endive, separated & washed

1 tablespoon of walnut oil

### Directions

1. On a cookie sheet, sprinkle the walnuts in a single layer and toast 10 to 15 minutes at 350 degrees F, stirring infrequently.

2. Add together the tofu, apple, flaxseed, curry powder, celery, oil, walnuts and ginger to a large bowl.

3. Place the endive in layers on salad plates. Ladle the apple-tofu mixture on it. Serve and enjoy.

# Dinner

## Tarragon Chicken Salad

*Any fresh or dried herb like fenugreek, chives, dill, and cumin to flavor the beans will do.*

Prep Time: 5 minutes

Cook Time: 0 minute

Serves: 2

### Ingredients:

8 oz. chicken breast, cooked & cut into 1" cubes

1 tablespoon walnut oil

3 cups of watercress bouquets, washed & separated

5 radishes, chopped

2 stalks celery, chopped

1 medium pear, diced

1/8 teaspoon cardamom

1/3 cup of whole pine nuts

1 tablespoon dried tarragon or 3 tablespoons of fresh and chopped tarragon

### Directions

1. Toss together all the ingredients in a large mixing bowl and serve.

## Snacks

Any of the snack ideas

# DAY 5

## Breakfast

### Creamy Dawn Millet Porridge
*A vegan, gluten-free and dairy-free rich anti inflammatory breakfast.*

Prep Time: 5 minutes

Cook Time: 40 minutes

Serves: 4

**Ingredients**

1 cup of millet, uncooked

½ cup raw almonds

1 cup almond milk

1 teaspoon of dairy-free vegan butter (Earth Balance)

1 teaspoon of maple syrup

2 tablespoon cinnamon

1 tablespoon carob powder

2 tablespoons ground flax seeds

2 tablespoons coconut flakes

¼ teaspoon almond extract

¼ teaspoon sea salt

**Directions**

1. Preheat oven to 375°F. Cook the millet as instructed on the package.

2. While it cooks, add together the almonds, butter, carob powder and maple syrup in a large bowl. Toss to coat well and then spread the mixture on a baking sheet that has been lined with parchment paper.

3. Bake until toasted or for about 30 minutes. Remove and set aside.

4. Remove also the cooked millet and transfer to serving bowls. Top with toasted almonds, almond milk, flax seeds, coconut flakes, almond extract and sea salt.

# Lunch

## Paprika Chicken Bake
*Enjoy lunch time with this baked delight.*

Prep time: 5 minutes

Cook time: 40 minutes

Serves: 4

**Ingredients:**

2 pounds of pumpkin, peeled and diced

2 pounds of chicken thighs and drumsticks pieces

¼ cup of pine nuts

4 tablespoons of olive oil

1 tablespoon of paprika powder

1 rosemary sprig

Pepper

Salt

**Directions:**

1. Preheat oven to 400°F.

2. Grease an oven dish and place the pumpkin and chicken pieces in it. Use a pastry brush to brush them with oil.

3. Sprinkle the paprika, pepper and salt over the pumpkin and chicken evenly. Add the sprig of rosemary.

4. Use a foil to cover the dish and place in the oven. Bake for 30 minutes.

5. Remove the foil, add the nuts and keep baking until the chicken is well-cooked.

# Dinner

## French Lentil Vegetable Soup

Prep time: 15minutes

Cook time: 20 minutes

Serves: 8-10

### Ingredients

1 pound dried French green lentils

4 cups (3 large onions) yellow onions, chopped

4 cups (2 leeks) chopped leeks, white part only

1 tablespoon (3 cloves) minced garlic

1/4 cup olive oil, plus more for drizzling on top

1-½ teaspoons freshly ground black pepper

1 tablespoon kosher salt

1 teaspoon dried thyme leaves or 1 tablespoon minced fresh

1 teaspoon ground cumin

3 cups (8 stalks) medium-diced celery

3 cups (4-6 carrots) medium-diced carrots

1/4 cup tomato paste

3 quarts chicken stock

2 tablespoons red wine or red wine vinegar

Freshly grated Parmesan cheese

## Directions

1. Add boiling water to a large bowl and let the lentils sit inside for 15 minutes. Drain.

2. In a large stockpot, sauté the onions, garlic and leeks with the olive oil, salt, pepper, cumin and thyme over medium heat for 20 minutes.

## Snacks

Any of the snack ideas

# DAY 6

## Breakfast

### Poached Egg & Salmon On Multigrain Toast

Prep Time: 5 minutes

Cook Time: 5 minutes

Serves: 1

**Ingredients**

Multigrain toast

Poached egg

Smoked salmon

Red onion and capers, sliced thinly

**Directions**

1. Placed the poached egg over the smoked salmon on your multi-grain toast.

2. Top with slices of red onion and capers

# Lunch

## Peppered Black-Eyed Peas Cold Salad

Prep Time: 5 minutes

Cook Time: 0 minute

Serves: 4

### Ingredients:

2 cans (30 oz.) organic black-eyed peas, drained & rinsed

4 teaspoons of poblano pepper

1/3 cup red onion, diced

7 stalks green onion or scallion, diced

¾ cup organic vegetable broth

1 clove fresh garlic

¼ teaspoon of fresh oregano,

1 tablespoon of extra virgin olive oil

2 tablespoon of lemon juice

3 tablespoon of fresh cilantro

¼ teaspoon of cayenne pepper

1/8 teaspoon of red pepper flakes, crushed

½ teaspoon of sea salt

### Directions:

1. Combine the pepper, onion, garlic, scallion or green onion, poblano pepper and black eye peas in a large bowl, mixing thoroughly.

2. In a small bowl, combine garlic, red pepper flakes, vegetable broth, cilantro, lemon juice, cayenne pepper, oregano and salt. Gradually whisk in the olive oil.

3. Gently pour the dressing over the black-eyed pea mixture, mixing thoroughly until it covers the black-eyed peas.

*Greens Salad*

# Dinner

## Italian Styled Chicken And Green Beans
*A quick and easy one-pot meal*

Prep Time: 5 minutes

Cook Time: 15 minutes

Serves: 1

### Ingredients:

3/4 cup green beans, cut in pieces of 1-inch

3/4 cup onions, chopped

3 oz skinless chicken breast, baked

2 teaspoons olive oil

1 (14.5 oz) can diced tomatoes

1 teaspoons bay leaf

Italian seasoning, to taste

Salt and pepper, to taste

### Directions

1. Steam or boil the green beans. Heat the olive oil in a saucepan and then add onion and sauté until tender.

2. Next, add chicken, tomatoes, Italian seasoning, bay leaf, salt and pepper. Cover and simmer 10 minutes.

3. Drain excess liquid from beans and then add it to the tomatoes and onion mixture. Cook 5 more minutes. Remove the bay leaf, serve and enjoy.

# Snacks

## Gingerbread Protein Balls

Prep Time: 30 minutes

Cook Time: minutes

Serves: 4

**Ingredients:**

1 cup walnuts, roasted

1 cup almonds, roasted

½ cup unsweetened desiccated coconut

1 teaspoon ground cloves

1 tablespoon ground ginger

1tablespoon chia seeds

2 tablespoons honey

**Directions:**

1. Blend all the ingredients in a food processor and blend until mixture comes together.

2. If dry, add some water.

3. Form mixture into balls, place in a container and refrigerate.

# DAY 7

## Breakfast

### Quinoa Chia Porridge

*Quinoa and nuts are loaded with anti-inflammatory properties and help to stabilize blood sugar. Cinnamon helps to build blood sugar as well as reduce inflammation. Cashew gives this breakfast its creamy look.*

Prep Time: 5 minutes

Cook Time: 10 minutes

Serves: 2

**Ingredients**

2 cups of cooked quinoa

1 cup of thick cashew milk

¼ cup toasted walnuts

2 teaspoons of ground cinnamon

1tablespoon of chia seeds

1 cup organic blueberries, frozen or fresh

2 teaspoon of raw honey

**Directions**

1. Combine the cashew milk and quinoa in a saucepan, set heat to medium low and slowly warm.

2. Add in the blueberries, walnuts and cinnamon, stirring until thoroughly warmed. Remove from heat and add the raw honey and stir. Top with the chia seeds.

3. Serve and top with raw cacao nibs.

# Lunch

## Leek & Parsley Soup

*Leeks which are high in vitamins contain kaempferol, a natural flavonol that's also found in broccoli, kale, and cabbage. Kaempferol are antioxidant, anti-inflammatory, antimicrobial, anticancer, cardioprotective and so much more!*

Prep Time: 15 minutes

Cook Time: 15 minutes

Servings: 4-6

### Ingredients

1 bunch of fresh flat-leaf parsley, stems separated& chopped (keep the parsley leaves for garnish)

2 large or 3 medium leeks, white & pale green parts chopped

1 tablespoons of olive oil

4 green onions, chopped

1 medium zucchini, unpeeled & shredded

4 cups of low-sodium chicken broth or 4 cups of water + 2 teaspoons salt

### Directions

1. In a large stockpot, heat the olive oil over medium-high heat.

2. Add the parsley stems and leeks. Cook and stir for 4-5 minutes.

3.  When the leeks lighten in color, add the green onions, zucchini and broth or water and then bring to a boil. Lower the heat; simmer 8 -10 minutes and cool for about 10 minutes.

4. Serve warm, garnished with fresh parsley leaves.

# Dinner

## Salmon And Quinoa With Tahini-Yogurt Sauce

Prep Time: 5 minutes

Cook Time: 10 minutes

Serves: 4

### Ingredients

1 cup white quinoa

1 medium carrot, peeled& thinly sliced

1 bunch kale, stems removed & thinly sliced

2 cups cooked chickpeas, rinsed & drained, if canned

2 tablespoons of lemon juice

2 garlic cloves, minced

1/4 cup dried cranberries, cherries or currants

Sea salt

Olive oil

1 tablespoon hemp seeds (optional)

4- 4-ounce sockeye salmon fillets, with skins

For The Sauce:

1/2 cup Greek yogurt

1/4 cup tahini paste

1 tablespoon lemon juice

1/2 cup water

1/2 teaspoon sea salt

## Directions

1. Add 2 cups of water and the quinoa to a medium saucepan and bring to a boil. Cover pan and cook 15 minutes on low heat. Uncover, fluff and set aside for 10 minutes.

2. Meanwhile, combine the carrots, 2 tablespoons of olive oil, lemon juice, kale, garlic and 1/2 teaspoon salt in a large mixing bowl. Toss the kale to coat in the oil and lemon.

3. To the kale mixture, add the cooked quinoa, dried fruit, chickpeas and hemp seeds (if using). Mix to incorporate and taste for seasoning.

4. In a large non-stick skillet, heat 2 tablespoons of oil. Pat-dry the salmon, season with salt and place the salmon skin-side down over high heat, cooking for 2 to 3 minutes until nicely browned.

5. Flip the fish carefully and cook 2 more minutes, until opaque up the sides. Serve the quinoa onto bowls and top with the seared salmon.

6. For the sauce, whisk all ingredients together until smooth, adding more water as necessary. Spoon the sauce over the fish and enjoy.

# Snacks

Any of the snack ideas

# DAY 8

## Breakfast

### Peach Quinoa With Nuts And Flax

*Allspice and hazelnuts, these rich and warming flavours enhance the delicious taste of this whole-grain cereal recipe.*

Prep Time: 5 minutes

Cook Time: 20 minutes

Serves: 4

### Ingredients

1 cup of dry quinoa

2 cup unsweetened soy milk

¼ teaspoon of ground allspice

1 ½ cups frozen peaches or 2 medium peaches, peeled & diced

2 tablespoons of ground flaxseeds, ground

2 tablespoons of chopped hazelnuts, chopped

Pinch sea salt, optional

### Directions

1. Combine peaches, soy milk, quinoa and allspice in a medium saucepan and bring to a boil, stirring often.

2. Cover pan and simmer on low until quinoa is tender or for about 20 minutes.

3. Top with the flaxseeds and hazelnuts.

# Lunch

## Baby Spinach& Dilled Egg Salad
*A superb way to enjoy more omega-3 fats.*

Prep Time: 20 minutes

Cook Time: 5 minutes

Serves: 2

### Ingredients

3 cups of fresh baby spinach, trimmed &washed

4 whole omega-3 eggs

2 tablespoons of fresh dill, finely chopped

2 tablespoons of scallions, finely chopped

1 large red apple, cut into wedges

2 tablespoons of organic soy mayonnaise

2 teaspoons Dijon mustard

Pinch sea salt

Dash freshly ground black pepper

### Directions

1. Cover eggs in a saucepan, cover with cold water, set heat to medium high and bring to a boil.

2. Remove, cover, and set eggs aside for 15 minutes. Drain and plunge eggs in ice water to cool.

3. Now peel and coarsely chop the eggs then combine with the dill, pepper, mustard, scallions, mayonnaise and salt in a medium bowl, tossing lightly.

4. Arrange the apple wedges and spinach on a plate, top with the egg salad and serve.

# Dinner

## Chicken With Italian Radicchio

*Radicchio is an Italian type of chicory with purple leaves that are streaked with white.*

Prep Time: 10 minutes

Cook Time: 20 minutes

Serves: 2

**Ingredients:**

2 cups radicchio

5 oz boneless skinless chicken breast, cut into strips

2 oz prosciutto

2 tablespoons balsamic vinegar

2 tablespoons sliced almonds, toasted

1/2 cup blueberries

2 peaches, pitted & sliced

1 cup strawberries

Salt, to taste

**Directions**

1. Preheat oven to 350°F. Sprinkle chicken with salt and place in a baking pan then cover with the radicchio and prosciutto.

2. Place in the oven for 15-20 minutes. Serve sprinkled with balsamic vinegar and almonds. Serve with peach and berry fruit salad.

# Snacks

## Cauliflower "Popcorn"
Prep Time: 5 minutes

Cook Time: 20 minutes

Serves: 1

### Ingredients

4 cups cauliflower, cut into large florets

2 teaspoons of olive oil

Kosher salt, to taste

### Directions

1. Toss the florets with olive oil to coat well then sprinkle with kosher salt.

2. Roast at 450°F for 25 to 30 minutes until soft and browned.

3. Serve drizzled with extra virgin olive oil.

# DAY 9

## Breakfast

### Inflammation- Soothing Green Blend

Prep Time: 10 minutes

Cook Time: 0 minute

Serves: 1

**Ingredients**

¼ medium pineapple, peeled

1 pear, any hard kind

1 lime, peeled

1 inch slice ginger

½ stick celery

¼ medium cucumber

1 floret cauliflower

½ medium ripe avocado

3 ice cubes

**Directions:**

1. Juice the pear, pineapple, ginger, lime, cucumber, cauliflower and celery.

2. Add the ice and avocado flesh to a blender.

3. Pour the juice to the blender and blend until smooth.

# Lunch

## Chicken & Grape Salad

*Use leftover chicken for this tasty lunch recipe*

Preparation time: 5 minutes

Cooking time: 5 minutes

Servings: 4

**Ingredients:**

1lb chicken, cooked leftover

1 cup red or green grapes, halved or left whole

2 boiled eggs, sliced

2 stalks celery, sliced

½ cup toasted pecans, chopped

2 large ripe tomatoes, diced

Flesh from 1 avocado, sliced

For Dressing

2 tablespoons olive oil

 2 tablespoons lemon juice

**Directions:**

1. Combine all the ingredients in a bowl and gently mix.

2. Drizzle with the dressing ingredients, tossing gently.

3. Serve and enjoy!

# Dinner

## Moroccan Chicken With Cauliflower And Cashews

*Garam masala is a mix of ground spices like cloves, mace, cumin, cardamom, fennel, nutmeg, coriander and black pepper.*

Preparation time: 5 minutes

Cooking time: 30 minutes

Serves: 4

**Ingredients:**

½ cup of raw cashews, chopped

1 tablespoon extra-virgin olive oil

1 lb. skinless, boneless chicken breasts, cut into 1" cubes

3 cloves garlic, pressed

1 small onion, chopped

2 cups of cauliflower florets

6 cups of low-sodium, organic chicken stock

2 cups of chickpeas, canned

1 tablespoon garam masala

2 tablespoon pomegranate molasses

**Directions**

1. Preheat oven to 350 degrees F. Add olive oil to an ovenproof casserole dish and set on medium-high heat.

2. Once heated, add chicken, brown and stir occasionally for 5 minutes. Add garlic, onions, cauliflower, chicken stock, chickpeas, garam masala, pomegranate and molasses.

3. Cover and place in oven to cook for about 25 minutes. Remove, top with chopped cashews and serve.

*Chicken Vegetable*

# Snacks

## Date Balls

*Those on a vegan and paleo diet will enjoy this easy treat.*

Prep Time: 1 hour15 minutes

Cook Time: 0minutes

Serves: 24 small cookies

**Ingredients:**

2 cups walnuts

1 cup unsweetened coconut, shredded

2 tablespoons coconut oil

2 cups of Medjool dates, soft &pitted

1 tsp vanilla extract

1/2 teaspoon of salt

**Directions:**

1. Place the coconuts and walnuts in a food processor and process until crumbly. Now add the dates, vanilla, coconut oil, and salt and then process a second time until the batter is a sticky and uniform.

2. Next, form balls by scooping the dough and roll between your hands. Arrange on a lined baking sheet then freeze 1-2 hours before serving, or seal properly before refrigerating.

3. To make a truffle, roll in cocoa powder or shredded coconut before chilling!

# DAY 10

## Breakfast

### Turmeric Apple Green Tea
*Enjoy this paleo, vegetarian, gluten-free and diary-free drink*

Preparation time: 5 minutes

Cooking time: 40 minutes

Yields: 5 cups

**<u>Ingredients</u>**

6 cups purified water

2 cinnamon sticks

3 organic green tea bags

2 large organic Fuji apples, cut into wedges

1 teaspoon organic turmeric powder

3-inch piece fresh ginger, peeled and cut into chunks

$\frac{1}{8}$ teaspoon of black pepper

$\frac{1}{8}$ teaspoon cayenne pepper

$\frac{1}{2}$ teaspoon pure vanilla extract

2 tablespoons fresh Meyer lemon juice

2 tablespoons raw honey

**<u>Directions:</u>**

1. Add the cinnamon sticks, apple wedges, ginger, turmeric, black pepper, cayenne and vanilla to a large saucepan of water. Stir, set at medium-high heat and bring to a boil.

2. Set heat to low and simmer for 30 minutes then add the green tea bags and stir well together. Let it simmer for another 3 to5 minutes to allow the tea to steep.

3. Now remove tea bags and add in the raw honey and lemon juice, stirring well. Strain the tea and pour into serving cups.

4. Enjoy hot. The cooked ginger and apples can also be eaten!

# Lunch

## Miso Soup

Prep time: 5 minutes

Cook time: 25 minutes

Serves: 4

### Ingredients

½ tablespoon of fresh parsley, chopped

2 carrots, sliced

2 tablespoons dried wakame, chopped

1 onion, sliced

1 cup tofu, organic and cubed

4 tablespoons miso

4 cups water

### Directions

1. Heat ½ cup of water in a large pot. Add onion and carrots and cook for 8 to 10 minutes.

2. Add ½ cup of water again and tofu and cook for another 5 to 7minutes. Add the remaining water and bring to a boil.

3. Reduce heat, cover and simmer 15 minutes.

4. Create a thin paste by adding 2 tablespoons of boiled water to miso in a small bowl. Add wakame, miso paste, and parsley to the pot and stir.

5. Cook another 5 minutes and serve.

# Dinner

## Steamed Salmon With Lemon & Zucchini

Prep Time: 10 minutes

Cook Time: 10 minutes

Serves: 4

### Ingredients:

4 (6 oz.) salmon fillets

1 onion, sliced

2 small zucchini, sliced

1 lemon, sliced

1/2 cup water

1 cup white wine

1/4 teaspoon freshly ground pepper

1/2 teaspoon kosher salt

### Directions

1. In a Dutch oven, place the lemon, onion, white wine, zucchini and water.

2. Season the fish with pepper and salt. Place an oiled steamer rack over the vegetables in the Dutch oven and set over medium-high heat to boil.

3. Lower heat to medium-low and place the seasoned fish on the rack. Cover and steam for about 10 minutes until cooked through.

4. Transfer veggies and liquid to plates, place fish on top and top with olives.

## Snacks

Any of the snack ideas

*Chocolate Nut Clusters*

# DAY 11

## Breakfast

### Chia Orange Avocado Smoothie

Prep time: 5 minutes

Cook time: 0 minute

Serves: 2

**Ingredients**

3 cups purified water

2 large oranges, peeled & cut into small pieces

1 medium avocado, seeded & peeled

¼ teaspoon cinnamon

½ teaspoon turmeric powder

1 teaspoon fresh grated ginger

2 cups organic spinach

2 tablespoons chia seeds

Pinch fresh ground black pepper

**Directions**

1. Place all the ingredients into blender and blend until it is smooth and creamy.

# Lunch

## Assorted Cabbage Soup

Prep time: 15 minutes

Cook time: 45 minutes

Serves: 2

### Ingredients

1/3 cup of garbanzo beans, rinsed &drained

6 oz ground turkey breast

2 teaspoons of olive oil

4 cups cabbage, shredded

3/4 cup onions, diced

1½ cups mushrooms, sliced

1 1/4 cups tomatoes, diced

1½ cups bell peppers, diced

2 cloves garlic, chopped

1/8 teaspoons of Tabasco sauce, to taste

1/8 teaspoons of caraway seeds, to taste

Salt and pepper, to taste

2 teaspoons of extra virgin olive oil, for drizzle

### Directions

1. Brown onion and meat in olive oil. Add all the ingredients but leave the extra virgin olive oil.

2. Cover and simmer about 30-40 minutes or until the veggies are cooked. Drizzle with olive oil.

# Dinner

## Ground Turkey & Vegetable Stuffed Peppers

*Why crave for the traditional beef and rice stuffed pepper, when you can enjoy a healthier dish of Stuffed peppers with ground turkey and vegetables.*

Prep Time: 35 minutes

Cook Time: 15minutes

Serves: 4

**Ingredients:**

4 red bell peppers

1 lb (93%) lean ground turkey

2 tbsp olive oil

1 cup sliced mushrooms

1/2 onion, minced

1 zucchini, chopped

1/2 yellow bell pepper, diced, tops cut off and deseed

1/2 green bell pepper, diced, tops cut off and deseed

1 cup fresh spinach

1 tablespoon tomato paste

1 (14.5 oz) can diced tomatoes, drained

1 tsp Italian seasoning

1/2 tsp garlic powder

Salt and pepper to taste

**Directions:**

1. Boil a large pot of water. Cook the cut and deseeded peppers (as well as the cut tops) in the boiling water for 5 minutes. Drain the water and set to one side.

2. Preheat oven to 350 degrees F.

3. Cook the turkey in a skillet until well- browned and remove then set aside.

4. Heat the olive oil in the same skillet and then add in the onions, zucchini, peppers, mushrooms and spinach, and let it cook until tender.

5. Place the turkey back to the skillet and add the rest of the ingredients. Stuff the peppers with the mixture

6. Put the peppers inside a casserole dish, replace tops (if you like), and leave it to bake for 15 minutes.

# Snacks
Any of the snack ideas

# DAY 12

## Breakfast

### Avocado Toast With Eggs

*Ghee is excellent for our digestive tract. When we have healthy gut, nutrients are better absorbed and toxins are eliminated. This helps to reduce inflammation. Avocado with its healthy fats protects against inflammation while eggs are loaded with protein that stabilize blood sugar.*

Prep Time: 5 minutes

Cook Time: 0 minute

Serves: 1

#### Ingredients

1 slice of toasted bread, gluten-free

½ avocado

½ teaspoon of ghee

1 egg, scrambled or poached

Handful of spinach

Red pepper flakes

#### Directions

1. Top the toasted gluten-free bread with glee and then spread the avocado unto it.

2. Place the spinach on top of the avocado and top with the egg, scrambled or poached.

3. Sprinkle over with the red pepper flakes and enjoy.

# Lunch

## Green Bean& Cherry Tomato Salad

Prep Time: 5 minutes

Cook Time: 2 minutes

Serves: 4

### Ingredients:

4 handfuls green beans, steamed lightly

1 cup cherry tomatoes, halved

¼ red onion, sliced

1 large carrot, grated coarsely

2 handfuls arugula leaves, chopped roughly

¼ cup pine nuts, toasted

3 tablespoons olive oil

¼ cup red wine vinegar

### Directions:

1. Add together all the ingredients in a serving bowl and gently toss.

2. Serve with chicken or seafood of choice.

# Dinner

## Braised Kale With Caramelized Onions, Walnuts And Goat Cheese

*This vegetarian recipe features some of the healthiest staples from the anti-inflammatory diet*

Prep Time: minutes

Cook Time: minutes

Serves: 4

### Ingredients:

2 bunches of Lacinato kale (1½- 2 pounds in total)

6 garlic cloves, finely minced

½ cup of Extra-Virgin olive oil, divided

1 cup water

2 tablespoons apple cider vinegar

2 medium (about 3 cups) yellow onions, thinly sliced

½ cup crumbled goat cheese

¾ cup raw walnut halves, chopped

Kosher salt and freshly ground black pepper

### Directions

1. Wash kale and shake off some excess water then cut in one inch, bite-sized pieces.

2. Heat ¼ cup of olive oil in a large pan over medium heat. Add minced garlic, cooking and stirring about 1 minute, until fragrant.

3. Add the chicken stock and vinegar; set heat to high. Add a handful of kale, stir and wilt as necessary, and then keep adding until all kale is inside the pot.

4. Cover pot and lower heat to medium-low. Cook about 25 minutes, stirring occasionally.

5. Meanwhile, add ¼ cup of olive oil to a separate saucepan and set over medium heat. Add onions, pinch of salt and pepper. Cook about 20 minutes until lightly browned, stirring infrequently.

6. Add walnuts and cook another 5 minutes. Stir walnuts, goat cheese crumbles and onions into kale. Season with salt and pepper and serve hot.

*Kale Salad*

## Snacks
Any of the snack ideas

# DAY 13

## Breakfast

### Fennel Pudding
*Fennel contains fiber which helps to fight inflammation*

Prep Time: 10minutes

Cook Time: 50minutes

Serves: 2

**Ingredients:**

171/2 ounce fennel, chopped coarsely

2 ounce onion, chopped finely

11/2 tbsp low fat butter

2 egg yolks

Salt

Water

**Directions:**

1. Add the chopped onion, fennel, water and butter to a pan, cover and braise covered until soft and the water evaporates.

2. Puree in a food processor and then set aside to cool.

3. Whisk the egg yolks and some salt together and then add to fennel puree, mixing well.

4. Butter a baking dish and add the mixture.

5. Finally, bake in a preheated oven or at 302° F for 20 to30 minutes.

# Lunch

## Salmon Orange Salad

*This recipe is loaded with protein; it is delicious too!*

Prep Time: 5minutes

Cook Time: 5minutes

Serves: 2

**Ingredients:**

1 cooked salmon fillet, flaked

1 orange, peeled & sliced

1 medium avocado, sliced

1 stalk celery, sliced

½ cup cherry tomatoes, halved

¼ red onion, sliced

¼ cup lime juice

2 tablespoons of olive oil

Salt and pepper, to taste

**Directions:**

1. Add all salad ingredients to a bowl

2. Top with olive oil and lime juice, mixing well.

# Dinner

## Spicy Butternut Squash With Fennel

Prep Time: 25minutes

Cook Time: 45minutes

Serves: 4

### Ingredients

1½ pound butternut squash

1 large onion, with root end, cut lengthwise into wedges of ½-inch-wide

1 fennel bulb, trimmed & cut across into wedges1-inch- wide

3 tablespoons olive oil

1 teaspoon ground cumin

1 teaspoon ground cinnamon

1 teaspoon chili powder

½ teaspoon turmeric

### Directions

1. Peel the squash and cut in half lengthwise. Seed, half crosswise, and then cut lengthwise into ¾-inch-wide wedges. Position the rack in bottom third of oven and preheat to 450° F.

2. Combine the squash, fennel and onion on a rimmed baking sheet. Add the oil and toss well to coat.

3. Add all the spices in a bowl and combine well. Sprinkle the spice mixture over veggies and toss to coat. Sprinkle with salt & pepper.

4. Roast about 45 minutes but turn only once, until veggies are tender and browned. Place on a shallow dish and serve.

# Snacks

## Oat Soufflé

Prep Time: 5minutes

Cook Time: 20minutes

Serves: 1

### Ingredients

2 tablespoons of walnuts, finely chopped

2/3 cup Egg Beaters, whites

1/4 cup skim milk

1/4 cup oat bran (ground steel cut oats)

1 teaspoons of cinnamon

1 teaspoons of vanilla extract

1/4 cup of blueberries

1 teaspoon of honey, for drizzle

### Directions

1. Combine all ingredients (except the honey and blueberries).

2. Place in a skillet, cover and cook over low heat until set. Turn the other side and cook until done.

3. Enjoy topped with blueberries and drizzle with honey.

# DAY 14

## Breakfast

### Flavored Poached Egg Bagel

Prep Time: 5minutes

Cook Time: 5minutes

Serves: 1

**Ingredients**

1 whole grain bagel

1 organic egg, poached or soft boiled

1 tablespoon of red onion, diced

1 teaspoon fresh basil, finely chopped

1 tablespoon salsa

Salt and pepper, to taste

**Directions**

1. Toast the whole grain basil and lay on a flat surface.

2. Top with the egg, red onion, fresh basil, salsa, salt and pepper to taste.

3. Serve and enjoy.

# Lunch

## Avocado And Tuna Salad

*A low carb anti-inflammatory lunch that's quick, easy and delicious!*

Prep Time: 15 minutes

Cook Time: 10 minutes

Serves: 1

**Ingredients:**

1 handful of arugula leaves

½ cup of cherry tomatoes, halved

½ medium avocado, diced

½ Lebanese sliced cucumber

2 tbsp of hemp seeds

5 oz can tuna (with brine), drained & flaked

2 tablespoons olive oil

1 tbsp lime juice or fresh lemon

**Directions:**

1. Mix all the salad ingredients together.

2. Drizzle with lime juice or lemon and olive oil.

# Dinner

## Wild Salmon With Sweet Potatoes, Rosemary & Lemon Asparagus

Prep Time: 15 minutes

Cook Time: 30 minutes

Serves: 2

### Ingredients:

8 oz. wild salmon, cut into two 4-ounce sizes

1 small yellow onion, washed & sliced¼" thick

2 small sweet potatoes, washed & sliced¼" thick

2 tablespoons of extra-virgin olive oil

1 garlic clove, pressed

2 teaspoons of dry mustard

1 tablespoon fresh rosemary, chopped

1 tablespoon lemon juice, freshly squeezed

½ pound fresh asparagus

Zest of 1 lemon

Pinch sea salt

### Directions:

1. Preheat oven to 425 degrees F. Line cookie sheet with parchment paper and lay the sliced onion and potato in a single layer on it. Drizzle with salt and olive oil and bake for 15 minutes.

2. Meanwhile, make a paste by mixing the garlic, lemon juice, rosemary and dry mustard and then set aside.

3. Remove onions and sweet potatoes from oven. Place the asparagus on the parchment paper next to the onion and sweet potatoes. Sprinkle the lemon zest on the asparagus.

3. Finally, lay the salmon on top of the onions and asparagus. Spread over mustard paste. Place sheet in oven and roast 12 minutes.

## Snacks
Any of the snack ideas

# DAY 15

## Breakfast

### Breakfast Burrito

Prep Time: 5 minutes

Cook Time: 15 minutes

Serves: 1

**Ingredients**

1 whole grain tortilla

½ cooked black beans

4 quartered cherry tomatoes

3 tablespoon of mashed avocado

2 tablespoon of plain hummus

Salt and pepper to taste

**Directions**

1. In a large skillet, toast a whole grain tortilla over medium heat.

2. Toast per side until golden brown and warm.

3. Transfer to a serving plate and top with the rest of the ingredients. Serve and enjoy.

# Lunch

## Cold Cucumber Soup

Prep Time: 15 minutes

Cook Time: 0 minute

Serves: 4-6

### Ingredients

1/2 cup chopped fresh parsley

6medium cucumbers, peeled, cut in half lengthwise, seeds removed & chopped

1 1/2 cups low-sodium chicken broth

Juice of 1 lemon

1 cup fat-free plain yogurt

1 1/2 cups fat-free half and half

Salt & freshly ground black pepper, to taste

Fresh dill, chopped

### Directions

1. Process the parsley, cucumbers and lemon juice in a food processor. Remove half of the puree and then set aside.

2. Add together the yoghurt, half and half and broth in a medium bowl. Add half of broth mixture to the puree in the food processor and then puree to mix well.

3. Season with salt and pepper. Remove to a container and chill. Repeat with the rest of the puree and broth mixture.

4. Stir and serve, garnished with fresh dill.

# Dinner

## Celery, Leek And Thyme Soup

*This adaptable soup can also be used as a base for any kind of vegetables. If you prefer, you could leave out the cashews and add a cup of coconut milk in its place. It is vegan, gluten-free, wheat-free, soy free and diary free.*

Prep Time: 15 minutes

Cook Time: 10 minutes

Serves: 4

### Ingredients

1 1/2 heads celery, sliced into chunks

1 leek chopped

4 cloves garlic, sliced

2 cardamom pods, seeds only

1 liter vegetable stock

2/3 cup cashew nuts

1 teaspoon of dried thyme

1 tablespoon of extra virgin olive oil

½ cup coconut milk

### Directions

1. Heat the oil in a pan and then add the leek, garlic, thyme, cardamom and celery and cook another 5 minutes.

2. Add stock, bring to a boil, lower heat and cook until the celery is tender.

3. Remove to a blender, add the nuts and cashew and blend until smooth.

4. Return the mixture to pan, add the coconut milk and warm through. Transfer to bowls and enjoy!

## Snacks
Any of the snack ideas

# DAY 16

## Breakfast

### Basil And Avocado Baguette

Prep Time: 2 minutes

Cook Time: 5 minutes

Serves: 1

**Ingredients**

2 slice whole grain baguette

1 small ripe avocado, mashed

1 teaspoon hot sauce

1 teaspoon fresh lemon juice

1 scallion, sliced

2 fresh basil leaves

Salt and pepper to taste

**Directions**

1. Toast the baguette and top with the rest of the ingredients.

2. Serve and enjoy

# Lunch

## Asian Bean Salad With Tangy Tahini Dressing

Prep Time: 10 minutes

Cook Time: minutes

Serves: 2

### Ingredients

Asian Bean Salad

 4 cup fresh baby spinach

 ¼ cup scallions, chopped

 ½ cup snow peas, strings removed

 1 cup canned adzuki beans, drained

 1 cup bean sprouts, rinsed & drained

Tahini Dressing:

 ¼ cup tahini

 2 tablespoons extra-virgin olive oil

 2 tablespoons lemon juice, freshly squeezed

 1 tablespoon garlic, minced

 Pinch sea salt

 Dash fresh black pepper

### Directions

1. Whisk together the garlic, tahini, lemon juice, olive oil, pepper and salt in a small bowl.

2. Add the spinach, snow peas, scallions, beans and bean sprouts to a large salad bowl.

3. Now pour the tahini dressing over it. Toss and enjoy

# Dinner

## Root Vegetable Tagine With Kale

Prep Time: 15 minutes

Cook Time: 35 minutes

Serves: 6-8

### **Ingredients**

2 tablespoons coconut or olive oil

1 large sweet onion, diced

2 large cloves garlic, minced

1 medium parsnip, peeled & diced

1 teaspoon ground cumin

½ teaspoon ground ginger

½ teaspoon ground cinnamon

1 teaspoon sea salt

3 tablespoons tomato paste

¼ teaspoon cayenne pepper

2 medium purple potatoes, peeled & diced

2 medium sweet potatoes, peeled & diced

2 bunches baby carrots, peeled

1 quart vegetable stock

2 cups kale leaves, roughly chopped

¼ cup of cilantro leaves, chopped roughly

2 tablespoons lemon juice

Pepitas or toasted slivered almonds, for serving (optional)

## Directions

1. Heat the oil in a stock pot. Sauté the onion for 5 minutes over medium-high heat until soft.

2. Add the parsnip and cook another 3 minutes until it starts to turn golden brown. Add the garlic, ginger, ground cumin, salt, cinnamon, tomato paste and cayenne. Stir and cook 2 minutes until very fragrant

3. Fold in the purple potatoes, carrots and sweet potatoes. Pour in the vegetable stock and bring to a boil. Set heat to medium-low and simmer, uncovered, about 20 minutes stirring infrequently, until the veggies are tender.

4. Stir in lemon juice and kale. Simmer 2 more minutes. Once the leaves slightly wilted remove and garnish with the cilantro and nuts, if using. Enjoy served over couscous or quinoa.

*Kale Salad*

# Snacks

## Crunchy Tamari Seeds

Prep Time: 15 minutes

Cook Time: 15 minutes

Serves: 2

**Ingredients**

2 teaspoons wheat-free Tamari

1 cup green unsalted pumpkin seeds

1 cup raw unsalted Sunflower seeds, shelled

**Directions**

1. Heat skillet over medium heat. Add the sunflower seeds, stirring frequently so it does not burn.

2. Transfer the seeds to a plate and sprinkle with 1 teaspoon of tamari. Stir to coat and set aside.

3. Put the pumpkin seeds in same hot skillet and toast, stirring frequently until slightly browned and puffed up. Remove skillet from heat.

4. Put on the same plate and add the remaining 1 teaspoon of tamari. Toss together until evenly coated.

5. Pour back into the hot skillet but do not return to heat, toss until dry. Let it cool and then store up to 2 weeks in an air-tight container.

# DAY 17

## Breakfast

### Blueberry-Cherry Smoothie

*Cherries, blueberries and kale are loaded with powerful anti-inflammatory properties that make this breakfast smoothie so worth it!*

Prep Time: 5minutes

Total Time: 5minutes

**Ingredients**

1 banana

1/2 cup of kale

1/4 cup of blueberries, frozen overnight

1 cup of cherries, pitted

1/2 teaspoon of turmeric

**Directions**

1. Prepare ingredients by washing the kale and tearing into bite-size pieces and pitting cherries.

2. Blend all ingredients in a blender and blend until smooth consistency. Enjoy!

# Lunch

## Roasted Veggie Salad

Prep Time: 15minutes

Cook Time: 45minutes

Serves: 4

### Ingredients:

2 tomatoes, cut in large chunks

1 red onion, cut in large chunks

1 green bell pepper, cut in large chunks

1 red bell pepper, cut in large chunks

2 beets, cubed

5 cloves garlic

1 sweet potato, peeled &cubed

1 teaspoon lemon pepper

1 tablespoon basil, sliced

2 cups romaine lettuce

2 teaspoons olive oil

### Directions:

1. Preheat oven to 425° Fahrenheit.

2. Add all the vegetables to the roasting pan and top with lemon pepper and basil.

3. Drizzle with olive oil and bake 45 minutes.

4. Divide the lettuce among four plates along with the veggie mixture. Serve and enjoy warm.

*Rich Vegetable Salad*

# Dinner

## Slow Cooker Turkey Chili

*Invite friends and family over for dinner and enable them have a feel of this tasty and healthy recipe.*

Prep Time: 10minutes

Cook Time: 4-6 hours

Serves: 8-10

**Ingredients:**

1 tbsp olive oil

1 lb 99% lean ground turkey

1 red pepper, chopped

1 medium onion, diced

1 yellow pepper, chopped

2 (15 oz) cans petite diced tomatoes

2 (15 oz) cans tomato sauce

2 (15oz) cans red kidney beans, rinsed and  then drained

2 (15 oz) cans black beans, rinsed and then drained

1 (16 oz) jar jalapeno peppers, drained

1 cup frozen corn

2 tbsp of chili powder

 1 tbsp of cumin

Salt and black pepper, to taste

For toppings: green onions, avocado, shredded cheese, sour cream/Greek yogurt (all optional)

Directions:

1. Brown the turkey in a heated skillet and transfer to slow cooker.

2. Add the rest of the ingredients.

3. Cover pot and cook on High temperature for 4 hours or on low heat for 6 hours. Serve with desired toppings.

# Snacks

## Apple Slices With Cinnamon
Prep Time: 2minutes

Cook Time: 0minute

Serves: 1

### Ingredients

1 medium apple, cored& sliced

1/4 teaspoon of ground cinnamon

### Directions

1. Place the sliced apple slices on a serving platter.

2. Sprinkle with cinnamon and serve.

# DAY 18

## Breakfast

### Almond Butter Berry Smoothie

Prep Time: 5minutes

Cook Time: minutes

Serves: 1

**Ingredients**

1/2 medium ripe banana

1/4 cup 1% low-fat milk

1 tablespoon of creamy almond butter

1 cup raspberries, fresh or frozen

1/2 cup crushed ice

**Directions**

Blend and enjoy!

# Lunch

## Mushroom Soup

*You will never go for can soup after this.*

Preparation time: 10 minutes

Cooking time: 37 minutes

Servings: 4

**Ingredients:**

20 stalks of fresh thyme, leaves removed

2 10-ounce packages of baby Portobello mushroom, sliced

2 10-ounce packages of white button mushroom, sliced

2 cups of unsweetened cashew or almond milk

2 cups of organic vegetable broth

2 tablespoons of tapioca flour

1 tablespoon of soy sauce or liquid aminos

2 large white onions, chopped

2 dried bay leaves

1 teaspoon of salt

Freshly ground black pepper

**Directions:**

1. Add the onions to a large saucepan, cover and sweat them for 5-7 minutes over medium heat.

2. Shift the onion to the pan sides and add the mushrooms to the center. Uncover and cook for 5 minutes.

3. Combine the mushrooms and onions together.

4. Add the thyme and keep cooking for at least 10 minutes.

5. Add the tapioca into the broth in a small bowl and stir until it is mixed and does not have lumps. Pour this mix into the mushrooms and stir to combine.

6. Add the milk to the pan and cook for at least 15 minutes while stirring occasionally.

7. Taste and season with salt and pepper.

# Dinner

## Cold Lemon Curry Squash Soup

*Enjoy this healthy, cooling, anti-inflammatory, hypoallergenic, gluten-free, and vegetarian and vegan soup.*

Prep Time: 15minutes

Cook Time: 20minutes

Serves: 4

### Ingredients

4 large summer squash, (yellow), chopped

1 large yellow onion, chopped

1 tablespoon coconut oil

3 cups+ water or vegetable stock

Juice of 1/2 - 1 lemon

3 medium cloves garlic, minced

1 teaspoon curry powder

Sea salt

Chopped parsley or cilantro to garnish

### Directions

1. Add coconut oil to a stock pot and set on medium heat. Add onion and garlic, sautéing about 5 minutes until translucent and fragrant.

2. Add summer squash and sauté 1 minute. Add the curry powder and stir 1 minute. Add water or vegetable stock and then heat to boiling.

3. Lower heat, cover pot and simmer over medium heat10-15 minutes until the summer squash are very tender.

4. Puree the soup with a stainless steel hand blender. Season with sea salt, pepper and lemon juice. Sprinkle with chopped parsley or cilantro. Serve soup hot or cold.

# Snacks

## Berry Freezer Pops
*Give yourself a summertime treat.*

Prep Time: 15minutes

Cook Time: minutes

Serves: 6

### Ingredients

1½ tablespoons of almonds

1 cup strawberries

3 cups plain low fat yogurt

### Directions

1. Combine almond and strawberries in a food processor and pulse until very small pieces.

2. Now add the yogurt and pulse 2-3 times. Divide the yogurt mixture equally in 6 small paper cups.

3. Put a Popsicle stick in the centre of the yogurt. Freeze overnight in the freezer. Peel the paper cup and eat.

# DAY 19

## Breakfast

### Granola Buckwheat & Ginger

*Mix this delicious recipe into a smoothie bowl or sprinkle over stewed fruit!*

Prep Time: 15minutes

Cook Time: 50minutes

Yield: 1 large container

**Ingredients**

2 cups of oats

1 cup of sunflower seeds

1 cup of buckwheat

1 cup of pumpkin seeds

1 cup of apple puree/sauce

1½ cups pitted dates

4 tablespoons of raw cacao powder

6 tablespoons of coconut oil

A piece of ginger, peel & grated

**Directions**

1. Pre-heat oven to 350 degrees F. Add the buckwheat, oats and seeds to a large mixing bowl and stir well.

2. Add the dates, apple puree and coconut oil to a saucepan and simmer 5 minutes or until the dates are soft. Then add the grated ginger.

3. Pour saucepan mixture in a blender, add the raw cacao powder and blend until smooth.

4. Pour the blended mix over the oat, seed and buckwheat mix and stir to coat well.

5. Spread the granola to 2 greased baking trays, place in the oven and bake 45 minutes. Remove trays after 15 minutes and stir well to prevent burns. Do this every 5-10 minutes till the 45 minutes are spent.

6. Once it's crispy, but not burnt, remove the granola from the oven and cool before placing it in an airtight container to store.


# Lunch

## Spinach, Walnut & Apple Lunch

Prep Time: 20 minutes

Cook Time: 5minutes

Serves: 4

**Ingredients:**

14 ounce spinach leaves, washed & spin-dry

1 heaped tablespoon of cranberries

2 garlic cloves, chopped finely

1 tablespoon olive oil

1.7 ounce walnut kernels

1/5 apple, sliced

Red peppercorns

Salt

**Directions:**

1. Fry the walnut kernels gently in the pan.

2. Add olive oil, garlic, and apple slices.

3. Add salt and peppercorns to your liking.

## Dinner

## Sautéed Spinach With Lemon And Garlic

Prep Time: 5minutes

Cook Time: 15 minutes

Serves: 2

### Ingredients

2 bunches fresh spinach (approximately2 lb.), washed

3 tablespoons of extra-virgin olive oil

4 medium garlic cloves, chopped

½ teaspoon of sea salt

½ teaspoon of freshly ground black pepper

Zest of 1 lemon (about ½ teaspoon)

### Directions

1. Add the extra-virgin olive oil to a large skillet and set over medium heat. Add the garlic and cook until golden.

2. Next, add the spinach, salt, and pepper, cooking and swirling, until the spinach is wilted. Remove from heat, add the lemon zest and stir. Serve and enjoy.

## Snacks

Any of the snack ideas

# DAY 20

## Breakfast

### Peachy Cardamom Quinoa Porridge

*Prepare healthy and delicious oat porridge with yummy peaches, cardamom, quinoa and non-diary almond milk.*

Prep Time: 3 minutes

Cook Time: 20 minutes

Serves: 2

**Ingredients:**

2 ripe peaches, sliced into slices

3 oz. quinoa

1 1/3 oz. porridge oats

4 cardamom pods

1 cup almond milk, unsweetened

1 tsp maple syrup

**Directions:**

1. In a small saucepan, combine the cardamom pods, oats and quinoa, then add 1 cup of water and ½ cup of almond milk. Bring the mixture to a boil, then gently simmer for 15 minutes, stirring often.

2. Now, pour in the rest of the almond milk then cook for another 5 minutes until it becomes creamy.

3. Take out the cardamom pods then scoop the porridge into jars or bowls; garnish with peaches and top with maple syrup.

# Lunch

## Coconut Banana Wrap

Prep Time: 2 minutes

Cook Time: 1-2 minutes

Serves: 1

### Ingredients

1 whole grain tortilla, toasted

2 tablespoon of walnut butter

1 banana, mashed or thinly sliced

1 tablespoon coconut flakes, toasted

Pinch sea salt

### Directions

1. Toast the tortilla in a large skillet over medium heat. Toast for 30 seconds per side until golden brown and warm.

2. Remove to a platter and spread with the walnut butter, banana and toasted coconut flakes.

3. Season with sea salt and serve.

# Dinner

## Baked Avocado Chicken And Vegetables

Prep Time: 10 minutes

Cook Time: 30 minutes

Serves: 1

### Ingredients:

3 oz boneless skinless chicken breast, sliced

1 tablespoon avocado, mashed

1 tablespoon low-fat cream cheese

1 cup zucchini, sliced

1 cup mushrooms, sliced

1/2 cup onions, chopped

3/4 cup green beans

1/4 cup unsalted vegetable stock

2 teaspoons dried basil

Salt and pepper - to taste

1 (14.5 oz) can diced tomatoes, with juice

1 tsp extra virgin olive oil, for drizzle

### Directions

1. Mix the mashed avocado with the cream cheese. Make a pocket with the sliced chicken. Put the avocado/ cream cheese mixture into this pocket and seal with a toothpick.

2. Place chicken in a baking tray, spray with olive-oil cooking spray and sprinkle with salt and pepper. Bake at 350° F for 20 to 25 minutes.

3. Next, spray a skillet with olive- oil spray. Sauté the veggies in 2 tablespoons of vegetable stock until crisp tender.

4. Add the diced tomatoes and heat through. Dish out the vegetables in a bowl drizzled with extra virgin olive oil. Put the chicken on another dish and enjoy.

## Snacks
Any of the snack ideas

*Macadamia Nuts*

# DAY 21

## Breakfast

### Apple Walnut Amaranth

*Rinse and soak the amaranth overnight to reduce the cooking time. The night before, put all the ingredients together (except the walnuts) in a saucepan and cover tightly, refrigerate, and cook in the morning.*

Prep Time: 10 minutes

Cook Time: 30 minutes

Serves: 4

#### Ingredients

1 cup of amaranth, dry

1 large apple, diced, with skin

3 cup of unsweetened gluten-free soy milk

¼ teaspoon of ground cinnamon

½ cup walnuts, chopped

Pinch sea salt, optional

#### Directions

1. Place the amaranth, apple, cinnamon and soy milk and in a saucepan, stir frequently and bring to a boil.

2. Cover and simmer on low for 25 to 30 minutes, until the amaranth is soft.

3. Top with walnuts and serve.

# Lunch

## Vegetable Scramble Wrap

Prep Time: 10 minutes

Cook Time: 10 minutes

Serves: 1

### Ingredients

1 (10oz) whole wheat flour tortilla

2 tablespoons green bell pepper, chopped

2 tablespoons red onion, chopped

3/4 cup liquid egg substitute

### Directions

1. Coat a skillet with cooking spray, place over medium heat and then add the onions and bell pepper, cooking and stirring, until softened.

2. Next, add the egg substitute. Cook and stir occasionally.

3. Ladle the egg mixture onto the tortilla, roll it up, serve and enjoy.

# Dinner

## Chicken Cordon Bleu

Prep Time: 20 minutes

Cook Time: 30 minutes

Serves: 2

### Ingredients:

4 teaspoons oat bran

5 oz boneless skinless chicken breast, pound to 1/4 inch thickness

3 tablespoons Dijon mustard (divided)

1 oz low-fat Swiss cheese, cut in half

1 oz extra-lean ham slice, cut in half

1/2 teaspoon agave nectar

1/2 cup unsalted chicken stock

2 teaspoons oat bran

1 tomato, sliced

4 cups broccoli, frozen

3 tablespoons 0%-Fat Greek yogurt

Salt and pepper, to taste

1 tablespoon extra virgin olive oil

Cooking spray

### Directions

1. Preheat toaster oven to 375°F then place 4 teaspoons of oat bran on plate and set aside. Combine 1 1/2 tablespoons of Dijon and agave in a bowl and set aside.

2. Place the ham and cheese on the chicken breast, roll up and secure with a toothpick. Coat the chicken in the mustard mixture and then in the oat bran. Spray olive oil on an aluminum foil sheet and place the chicken it. Bake 20 to 25 minutes.

3. Meanwhile to make the sauce, steam the broccoli. Whisk together stock and 1 teaspoon of oat bran until dissolved and cook over medium-high heat. Whisk until the mixture thickens.

4. Set heat to low and whisk in yogurt and the mustard that's left. Drizzle extra virgin olive oil, salt and pepper over the broccoli and tomato. Serve with chicken and sauce.

## Snacks
Any of the snack ideas

# DAY 22

## Breakfast

### Low-Fat Breakfast Veggie Bake
*Prepare a homemade low-fat veggie bake right in your oven.*

Prep Time: 15 minutes

Cook Time: 30 minutes

Serves: 4

**Ingredients:**

4 large field mushrooms

8 tomatoes, halved

4 eggs

1 garlic clove, sliced thinly

7 oz. bag spinach

2 tsp olive oil

**Directions:**

1. Heat up the oven to 356°F. Place each mushroom and the tomatoes in 4 ovenproof dishes.

2. Share the garlic amongst the dishes then sprinkle the oil on top. Add some seasoning then bake for 10 minutes.

3. In the meantime, place the spinach in a large colander, then pour in a kettle of boiling water to wilt it.

4. Squeeze out water from the spinach then add it to the dishes. Create a small space between the veggies then break an egg into each dish.

5. Place the dish in the oven again and cook for another 8 to 10 minutes or until the egg is well cooked to your taste.

*Healthy Salad Lunch*

# Lunch

## Tuna Pasta Salad

Serves: 2

Prep Time: 5 minutes

Cook Time: 6-8 hours

### Ingredients:

1 (6-ounce) can albacore tuna in water, drained

2 cups cooked whole wheat pasta

1/2 cup diced red bell pepper

1/2 cup diced celery

1/4 cup of cholesterol-free mayonnaise

Salt and freshly ground black pepper, to taste

### Directions:

1. Combine the tuna, pasta, bell pepper, celery, mayonnaise, salt and pepper in a bowl.

2. Cover and chill 6-8 hours.

# Dinner

## Chicken And Vegetable Medley

*Enjoy five different vegetables.*

Serves: 2

### Ingredients:

4 cups cauliflower, cooked

6 oz boneless chicken breast

3/4 cup onion

2 cups green beans

2 cups celery, chopped

2 cups mushrooms, chopped

1 green peppers, chopped

1/4 cup unsalted vegetable stock

1 tablespoon olive oil, divided

2 s dry onion flakes

2 teaspoons poultry seasoning

1 pear, 1/2 each

Salt and pepper, to taste

1 teaspoon slivered almonds

### Directions

1. Preheat oven to 350°F. Combine veggies, stock, seasonings, almonds and 2 teaspoons of olive oil in a casserole dish.

2. Rub 1 teaspoon of olive oil over chicken. Sprinkle with salt and pepper, place on top of vegetable dressing, cover and bake 30 minutes.

# Dinner

## Baked Tilapia With Vegetables

Prep Time: 5 minutes

Cook Time: 20- 25 minutes

Serves: 1

### Ingredients:

3 oz Tilapia

3/4 cup tomato, sliced

3/4 cup bell pepper, sliced

1½ cups zucchini, sliced

3/4 cup red onion, sliced

1½ cups summer squash, sliced

1 1/2 teaspoons of extra virgin olive oil

Herbs, of choice

Cooking spray, olive oil

Kosher salt and pepper, to taste

### Directions:

1. Preheat oven to 350°F. Spray bakeware with cooking oil and place the fish in it along with the chopped vegetables. Sprinkle with kosher salt and pepper and spray with olive oil.

2. Add preferred fresh herbs and bake for 20- 25 minutes. Put on plate and drizzle with extra virgin olive oil.

# Snacks

## Olive Tapenade And Raw Vegetables

*This tasty tapenade spread can be served with your fav veggies.*

Prep Time: 5 minutes

Cook Time: 20 minutes

Serves: 6

### Ingredients

½ cup of green olives, pitted

½ cup of kalamata olives, pitted

½ cup of roasted garlic cloves

1 tablespoon extra-virgin olive oil

1 tablespoon lemon juice, freshly squeezed

### Directions

1. Add together all ingredients in a food processor and puree until smooth.

2. Roast the garlic by preheating oven to 350 degrees F then placing garlic on a parchment paper—lined cooking sheet. Bake until light brown or for about 20 minutes.

# DAY 23

## Breakfast

### Chinese Veggie Omelet
*You can use your favorite vegetables for this omelet to suit your taste.*

Prep Time: 3 minutes

Cook Time: 5 minutes

Serves: 1

**Ingredients:**

¼ cup of chopped kale

¼ cup of chopped green onion

¼ cup of chopped tomato

1 tablespoon of low fat sour cream

2 eggs

1 teaspoon of garlic, crushed

¼ cup of chopped mushroom, optional

¼ cup of chopped bell pepper, optional

1/8 cup of chopped serrano pepper, optional

**Directions:**

1. In a bowl, whisk the eggs and sour cream together until it becomes light and fluffy.

2. Sauté the kale, green onion, tomato, kale, mushroom, and peppers lightly in a nonstick pan set over medium heat for about 2-3 minutes just until it becomes soft.

3. Add in the egg mixture and cook for 2-3 minutes or until you can use a spatula to lift the omelet sides from the pan.

4. Flip the omelet gently and cook for an additional 1 minute.

5. Fold the omelet in half gently and cook for 30 seconds per side.

# Lunch

## Salmon, Spinach And Blueberries Salad
*Insanely delicious and healthy.*

Prep Time: 10 minutes

Cook Time: 0 minute

Serves: 2

**Ingredients:**

8 ounces of smoked salmon, coarsely chopped

4 cups of mixed greens or baby spinach

½ cup of fresh blueberries

¼ cup of light blue or feta cheese, crumbled

½ red onion, sliced thinly

¼ cup of chopped walnuts, optional

1 avocado, peeled, pit removed and chopped

**Directions:**

1. Combine all the ingredients together and toss with vinaigrette.

# Dinner

## Rich Bean Soup

*Beans, onion, broccoli and garlic are the anti-inflammatory ingredients in this delicious soup recipe.*

Prep Time: 15 minutes

Cook Time: 60 minutes

Serves: 6

### **Ingredients**

1 cup canned navy beans, rinsed &drained

1 cup canned kidney beans, rinsed & drained

2 carrots, peeled and quartered lengthwise

2 small yellow squash, cut into 1/2-inch slices

2 large potatoes, rinsed& diced in large pieces

2 teaspoons minced thyme leaves

1 tablespoon olive oil

1 medium onion, chopped

2 medium Roma tomatoes, chopped

2 tablespoons garlic, minced

2 quarts vegetable stock

2 cups broccoli florets

1 bay leaf, crumbled

Kosher salt

Freshly ground black pepper

## Directions

1. Preheat oven to 350 degrees Fahrenheit.

2. Combine olive oil, salt and pepper in a large bowl, whisking well. Add the carrots, squash, garlic, potatoes and onion, tossing well to coat.

3. Place the coated veggies on a sheet pan and roast for 20 to 25 minutes.

4. Meanwhile, add the beans, stock, thyme and bay leaf in a large stock pot and set over medium heat, cook and stir occasionally for 10 minutes.

5. Pulse the stock and bean mixture with a hand blender until the beans are a little pureed.

6. Remove veggies from oven, add to pot and then stir in the tomatoes and broccoli. Cook 30-35 minutes until cooked through.

# Snacks

## Blueberry Almond Crisp

Prep Time: 10 minutes

Cook Time: 30 minutes

Serves: 6

Serving Size- 1 cup

## Ingredients

4 cups frozen blueberries

1/3 cup sliced almonds

1 cup white rice flour

¼ cup plus 2 tablespoons brown rice syrup (divided)

¼ cup olive oil

½ teaspoon salt

1 teaspoon cinnamon

2 teaspoons vanilla extract (alcohol- free)

2 tablespoons water

## Directions

1. Preheat the oven to 350° F. Mix flour and salt in a medium bowl. Add ¼ cup of the rice syrup and the oil then mix thoroughly. Add the nuts, stir and set aside.

2. In another bowl, add together the water, vanilla, cinnamon and 2 tablespoons of rice syrup. Set aside.

3. In a 9" x 13" pan, place the blueberries and pour the liquid mixture over. Gently toss to evenly coat the blueberries.

4. Spread the flour and the nut mixture evenly over the blueberries and cover with foil. Bake for about 20 minutes.

5. Next, increase oven temperature to 425° F, uncover and bake 10 more minutes. Once the topping is golden brown and crisp, it is done.

# DAY 24

## Breakfast

### Berry, Watermelon& Ginger Smoothie

Prep Time: 10 minutes

Cook Time: 0 minute

Serves: 1 large or 2 small servings

**Ingredients**

1 heaping cup watermelon chunks

1½ cups mixed berries, frozen

1 inch piece ginger, peeled &chopped or grated

2 teaspoons chia seeds

¾ cup coconut water

¼ Hass avocado

**Directions**

Blend all the ingredients and serve.

# Lunch

## Leek And Mushroom Soup

Prep Time: 25 minutes

Cook Time: 20 minutes

Serves: 4

**Ingredients:**

4 cups of chicken or vegetable stock

12 medium-size Swiss brown mushrooms, sliced

2 tablespoons of olive oil or ghee

3 bay leaves

2 garlic cloves, minced

½ ounce of dried porcini mushrooms

2 medium-size potatoes, peeled and diced

1 tablespoon of dried thyme leaves

2 large-size carrots, chopped

1 leek, sliced, tough ends discarded

Pepper

Salt

**Directions:**

1. Put the dried mushrooms in a bowl and cover with boiling water. Leave to soak for 20 minutes.

2. Heat the olive oil over medium heat in a large pot. Add the garlic and leek, sauté until tender.

3. Add in the carrots, potatoes and thyme to the pot. Cook and stir for 2 minutes.

4. Add the rest of the ingredients and allow the soup boil.

5. Turn down the heat to low and leave the soup to simmer until the veggies are soft.

# Dinner

## Quinoa With Snap Peas And Scallions

Prep Time: 5 minutes

Cook Time: 15 minutes

Serves: 4

**Ingredients**

3 cups quinoa

1 bunch scallions, white & green parts separated, thinly sliced

2 medium carrots, diced

1 cup snap peas, thinly sliced

2 tablespoons Organic Extra Virgin Coconut Oil

2 garlic cloves, minced

1 small yellow onion, diced

1 tablespoon minced fresh ginger

2 teaspoons toasted sesame oil

3 tablespoons Liquid Aminos

1 teaspoon sriracha

1 tablespoon Organic Shelled Hemp Seed

2 organic eggs, beaten

**Directions**

1. Heat the coconut oil in a large skillet. Sauté the onion, white scallion and carrot for about 5 minutes over high heat until soft and just brown.

2. Add the garlic, snap peas, green scallions and ginger. Stir-fry another 2 minutes until fragrant.

3. Add the quinoa, fold in and stir-fry 2 minutes to coat well in the veggie mixture. Once it begins to toast, add the sesame oil, sriracha and liquid aminos and stir to combine.

4. Push the quinoa to the side of the pan to create a well. Now, pour the eggs into the center, cooking and stirring lightly, until nearly set.

5. Toss the quinoa with the hemp seeds and eggs. Remove the quinoa to bowls and enjoy.

## Snacks
Any of the snack ideas

# DAY 25

## Breakfast

### Basil Egg Breakfast

*Enjoy this delicious anti-inflammatory breakfast that contains zero wheat, diary or heavy sugars. It is a mix of fresh veggies and herbs with eggs and bread that is gluten-free for a sumptuous meal.*

Prep Time: 5 minutes

Cook Time: 0 minute

Serves: 1

**Ingredients**

1 tomato, sliced

1 piece bread, gluten-free and toasted

1 hard-boiled egg, sliced

Olive oil

Fresh basil to taste

Salt and pepper

**<u>Directions</u>**

1. Place the toast on a plate and then drizzle toast with olive oil. Add the sliced tomato, basil as well as the egg on top of the toasted bread.

2. Drizzle again with olive oil, and then add salt and pepper to taste.

# Lunch

## Detox Broccoli Soup
*Green, delicious and comforting.*

Prep Time: 10 minutes

Cook Time: 15 minutes

Serves: 6

**Ingredients:**

2 cups of low sodium vegetable broth or filtered water

2 cups of broccoli florets

1 cup of greens

1 tablespoon of chia seeds

2 celery stalks, chopped finely

2 cloves of garlic, minced

1 carrot, peeled and chopped finely

1 onion, finely chopped

1 parsnip, peeled and chopped finely

Juice of ½ a lemon

1 teaspoon of coconut oil

½ teaspoon of sea salt

1 teaspoon of coconut milk, garnish

Mixed nuts and seeds, toasted

**Directions:**

1. Heat the oil in a soup pot over low heat and sauté the onion, parsnip, garlic, broccoli, carrot, and celery sticks for 5 minutes. Stir frequently.

2. Add the broth and allow to boil. Cover the pot and leave to simmer for 5-7 minutes until the vegetables are soft but not mushy.

3. Add the greens and stir. Transfer the soup to a blender, add the lemon and chia seeds and blend into a smooth cream.

4. Top the soup with the nuts and seeds.

# Dinner

## Healthy Salmon Chowder

Preparation time: 15 minutes

Cooking time: 30 minutes

Servings: 6

**Ingredients:**

1 tbsp canola oil

1/3 cup diced celery

1/3 cup diced carrot

4 cups low-sodium chicken broth

1½ cups water

1 (12 oz) salmon fillet, skinned (preferably wild-caught)

2½ cups of cauliflower florets, frozen, thawed then roughly chopped

3 tbsp diced fresh chives/scallions, (or 1½ tbsp dried chives)

2 cups of leftover mashed potatoes (or 1 1/3 cups of instant potato flakes, mashed)

¼ cup diced fresh dill (or 2 tsp of dried tarragon)

1 tbsp Dijon mustard

Freshly ground pepper to taste

¼ tsp salt

**Directions:**

1. Pour oil into a large-sized saucepan then heat over medium heat.

2. Add the celery and carrot then cook for 3 to 4 minutes, stirring often until the veggies start to brown.

3. Add water, the broth, salmon, chives/scallions and cauliflower then bring to a simmer.

4. Cover the pan then cook for 5 to 8 minutes, maintaining a gentle simmer, until the salmon is just cooked.

5. Transfer the salmon to a clean cutting board then use a fork to flake the fish into bite-size pieces.

6. Stir the mashed potatoes or potato flakes, dill/tarragon and mustard into the soup until well combined and then return to a simmer.

7. Add the salmon pieces then reheat. Season with pepper and salt, serve.

# Snacks

## Green Bean Stix
*Beans and cheese used as dippers.*

Prep Time: 2 minutes

Cook Time: 0 minute

Serves: 1

### Ingredients

1/3 cup salsa

20 green beans (or 3/4 cup), washed

1 low-fat cheddar Sargento cheese stick

### Directions

1. Cut off the ends of the green beans and then dip the beans and cheese into the salsa.

# DAY 26

## Breakfast

### Blueberry Almond Oatmeal
Prep Time: 5 minutes

Cook Time: 30 minutes

Serves: 1

**Ingredients:**

1 cup of water

¼ cup of no-fat milk

¼ cup of steel-cut oats

1/3 cup of frozen or fresh blueberries

1 tablespoon of almonds

1 teaspoon of ground flaxseed

**Directions:**

1. Boil the water over high heat.

2. Add the oats to the boiling water and cook for 25 minutes until the oatmeal becomes soft, while stirring regularly.

3. Turn down the heat to low and cook, stirring for an extra 3 minutes.

4. Add in the remaining ingredients, combine together and serve.

# Lunch

## White Beans On Greens

Prep Time: 15 minutes

Cook Time: 0 minute

Serves: 2

### Ingredients

6 cups of fresh baby mixed greens

2 cups of canned white beans, drained

½ cups of flat-leaf parsley, chopped

3 tablespoons of lemon juice, freshly squeezed

1 clove garlic, pressed

2 tablespoons of extra-virgin olive oil

Dash freshly ground black pepper

Pinch sea salt

### Directions

1. Combine beans with all the ingredients except the greens in a medium bowl.

2. Divide the greens between 2 plates and serve white bean mixture on it

# Dinner

## Roasted Salmon With Orange-Herb Sauce

Prep Time: 15 minutes

Cook Time: 0 minute

Serves: 6

### Ingredients

6 3-ounce skinless salmon fillets

1 large orange, unpeeled, sliced

1 1/2 tablespoons olive oil

1 large onion, halved, thinly sliced

3 tablespoons fresh dill, chopped

1 1/2 tablespoons fresh lemon juice

1/4 cup green onions, thinly sliced

1/2 cup orange juice

Extra unpeeled orange slices

### Directions

1. Preheat oven to 400°F. In a 13x9x2-inch glass baking dish, place the orange slices in a single layer, top with the onion slices, and drizzle with oil then sprinkle with salt and pepper. Roast until the onion is brown and tender and then remove.

2. Set oven temperature to 450°F. Place the onion and orange slices to the side of the baking dish and place the salmon in the center.

3. Sprinkle with 1½ tablespoons of dill, salt, pepper and the onion and orange slices atop. Roast about 8 minutes until the salmon is opaque in the center.

139

4. Meanwhile in a small bowl, combine orange juice, lemon juice, green onions and the dill that's left.

5. Remove fish to platter and add onion on the side; throw away the roasted orange slices and pour orange sauce over salmon. Garnish with extra orange slices.

# Snacks

## Roasted Cumin Carrots
*Maximize all the benefits from carrots with this crunchy snack.*

Prep Time: 10 minutes

Cook Time: 30 minutes

Serves: 4

**Ingredients:**

1 pound of carrots, peeled

1½ tablespoons of ghee

½ tablespoon of ground cumin

¼ teaspoon of salt

½ teaspoon of dried oregano

**Directions:**

1. Preheat oven to 400°F.

2. Divide the carrots in halves and cut in halves again lengthwise.

3. Arrange the carrot pieces on a greased or lined baking tray.

4. In a small bowl, combine the butter with cumin, salt and oregano. Brush this mixture over the carrots until they are well coated.

5. Roast the carrots for 15-30 minutes or until it is tender and browned lightly

# DAY 27

## Breakfast

### No-Dairy Cornmeal Breakfast

Prep Time: 5 minutes

Cook Time: 5minutes

Serves: 1

**Ingredients:**

1-1/2 cups unsweetened almond milk

1 cup corn meal (prefer corn grits)

2 cups cold water

Salt

Grapeseed oil

Pure maple syrup (to taste)

**Directions:**

1. Heat the almond milk in a saucepan.

2. In a bowl, add together corn meal and cold water, stirring well. Now add to the milk in saucepan and stir once more.

3. Bring to a boil and stir a few times. Lower heat and stir often to prevent it from sticking.

4. Once thick, remove from heat and then season with salt, grapeseed oil and maple syrup.

# Lunch

## Red Pepper Soup

Serves: 6

### Ingredients

1/4 cup dry white wine

12 large red bell peppers, cut into 1-inch pieces

5 cloves chopped garlic

4 teaspoons of olive oil

3 1/2 cups chopped onions

2 cups unsalted vegetable stock

2 teaspoons dried thyme

Salt and pepper, to taste

Red pepper flakes, to taste

6 tablespoons of 0%-Fat Greek yogurt

### Directions

1. Heat the oil in a stock pot or Dutch oven. Add onion and cook 3-4 minutes.

2. Once the onion softens, add garlic and cook 1more minute. Add wine and let it cool down to 1-2 tablespoons.

3. Next, add stock, peppers and spices and bring to boil. Set heat to low, cover and simmer about 30 minutes or until peppers are tender.

4. Place in food processor and puree, until smooth. Top with 1tablespoon yogurt sprinkled with thyme.

# Dinner

## Grilled Salmon Teriyaki

Prep Time: 15 minutes

Cook Time: 5minutes

Serves: 2

### Ingredients:

2 (8-ounce) salmon fillets

2 tablespoons of teriyaki sauce

1/2 teaspoon black pepper, coarsely ground

### Directions:

1. Place the salmon fillets in a bowl and pour over the teriyaki sauce; cover and set aside for 10 minutes.

2. Spray grill with cooking spray and heat to 450 degree F.

3. Take out the salmon from the marinade and rub the skinless side with the black pepper.

4. Place skin side up on the grill, and cook salmon over medium-high heat for about 4 minutes. Flip and cook another 2 minutes. Serve and enjoy.

# DAY 28

## Breakfast

### Beet & Strawberry Spicy Smoothie
Prep Time: 2-3 hours

Cook Time: 1 hour

Serves: 2

**Ingredients**

2/3 cup beet, roasted, chopped & frozen

2 cups ripe strawberries, chopped & frozen

1 teaspoon fresh ginger, peeled & grated

1 teaspoon fresh turmeric, peeled & grated

½ cup orange juice

1 cup unsweetened almond milk

Full-fat coconut milk, optional for serving

Goji berries, optional for serving

Raw cashews, optional for serving

**Directions**

1. Roast or steam the beet. Chop it into ½" pieces, wrap in foil, and bake in the oven at 400 degrees F for 45- 50 minutes. Alternatively, chop the beet in half and steam for 15- 20 minutes.

2. Once beet is cooked, let it cool and then measure 2/3 cup and place in the freezer for 2-3 hours. (Save extra roasted beet for salads).

3. Add all the ingredients to a blender and blend to complete smoothness.

4. Serve with coconut milk and goji berries.

# Lunch

## Broccoli Tuna

Prep Time: 15 minutes

Cook Time: 0minute

Serves: 1

**Ingredients:**

2 cups Broccoli, thinly chopped

3 oz tuna in water, drained

1 teaspoons of walnuts, chopped

1/2 teaspoons of Mrs. Dash Extra Spicy

1 teaspoon of Extra virgin olive oil

**Directions**

1. Combine tuna, broccoli and seasoning.

2. Serve sprinkled with walnuts and drizzled with extra virgin olive oil.

# Dinner

## Celery Soup

*Although celery is renowned for its ability to lower blood pressure, it also helps to fight against inflammation and aids in digestion.*

Prep Time: 35 minutes

Cook Time: 25minutes

Servings: 4-6

### Ingredients

1 bunch celery (about 7 cups), chopped

1 tablespoon olive oil

1 medium russet potato, peeled and cut into cubes

1 medium leek, (chop off white and pale green part, discard the dark green tops)

4 green onions (whites), chopped

4 cups low-sodium chicken broth or 4 cups water + 2 teaspoons salt

1 cup fat-free plain yogurt

Fresh parsley, chopped

### Directions

1. Heat the oil over medium-high heat. Add the onions, leek and celery, and cook for 8 to 10 minutes, stirring until beginning to soften.

2. Next, add the potato and broth or water and bring to a boil. Lower heat and simmer for 8 to 10 more minutes. Once the potato is tender, allow it to cool for about 10 minutes.

3. Pour the yogurt into the soup and stir. Blend or puree the soup in batches then pass through a strainer.

4. Serve warm or chilled sprinkled with parsley.

*Red Pepper Soup With Pear*

**Snacks**
Any of the snack ideas

# DAY 29

## Breakfast

### Sweet & Spicy Blast

*For those experiencing the pains and aches of inflammation, this sweet and spicy blast is just perfect.*

Prep Time: 5 minutes

Cook Time: 0minutes

Serves: 1-2

### Ingredients

½ cup Cherries

½ cup Lacinato Kale

½ banana

¼ teaspoon cinnamon

½ teaspoon turmeric

1 inch ginger

1 tablespoon chia seeds

1½ cups of coconut water

### Directions

1. Add all the ingredients to a tall cup and extract until smooth. *Enjoy!*

# Lunch

## Carrot Soup

Prep Time: 20minutes

Cook Time: 20 minutes

Servings: 1

**Ingredients:**

1 ounce fresh ginger, peeled & chopped finely

7 ounce carrots, washed, peeled &sliced thinly

2 tbsp butter

1/2 tbsp sugar

11|4 cup vegetable stock

1|4 cup Coconut milk

Salt and pepper to taste

**Directions:**

1. Cook the ginger and carrots in butter and sprinkle over with sugar.

2.  Add the stock and coconut milk and bring to boil.

3. Simmer over medium heat for about 20 minutes, and then blend for a smooth consistency.

4. Season with salt and pepper.

# Dinner

## Mediterranean -Flavored Tofu With Herbs And Sautéed Spinach

*This balsamic marinated tofu cooks to a beautiful brown color with crispy edges. Give some time to press and also drain the tofu before cooking.*

Prep Time: I hour 15 minutes

Cook Time: 15minutes

Serves: 4

### **Ingredients**

For The Tofu

1 (14-oz.) package extra-firm tofu, cut into 2

4 tablespoons of extra-virgin olive oil

1 teaspoon of minced rosemary

1 teaspoon of minced thyme

¼ teaspoon of sea salt

2 tablespoons of balsamic vinegar

1 teaspoon of minced garlic

1 teaspoon of minced parsley

½ teaspoon of coarsely ground black pepper

### **Directions**

1. Slice each cut piece of tofu horizontally, in half, to make 4 slices.

2. Drain the tofu by placing the slices in one layer on a shallow tray and then placing paper towels on top and underneath the tofu. Next, place

another tray on top of the tofu and use a heavy skillet to weigh it down. Refrigerate 30-60 minutes.

3. Meanwhile, add together garlic, 2 tablespoons extra-virgin olive oil, rosemary, vinegar, thyme, parsley, salt and pepper.

4. After draining the tofu, discard the excess liquid and pat dry. Place the tofu in a dish and pour the balsamic marinade over it. Chill at least 30 minutes.

5. Heat the remaining extra-virgin olive oil in a skillet over medium-high heat. Cook the tofu for 2-3 minutes per side, until brown. Transfer to a plate. Serve topped with sautéed spinach with lemon and garlic.

# Snacks

## Roasted Cauliflower With Turmeric
*An antioxidant-rich side dish you'll enjoy*

Prep Time: 10 minutes

Cook Time: 30minutes

Serves: 4

**Ingredients:**

1 medium head cauliflower, cut into florets

2 tbsp olive oil

2 tsp ground turmeric

Salt and pepper, to taste

**Directions:**

1. Preheat the oven to 350°Fand then line an oven tray.

2. Brush the florets with olive oil to cover well. Sprinkle with turmeric, salt and pepper.

3. Place in preheated oven and roast until lightly golden.

*Carrot Soup*

# DAY 30

## Breakfast

### Apple Oatmeal

*Combine your oat with apples and say goodbye to the doctors.*

Prep Time: 5 minutes

Cook Time: 20 minutes

Serves: 1

**Ingredients:**

½ cup of old-fashioned rolled oats

1 medium-sized cooking apple, core removed and diced

2 tablespoons of raisins

½ tsp cinnamon

A pinch of salt

**Directions:**

1. Preheat oven to 350°F.

2. In a small baking dish, thoroughly mix all the ingredients together.

3. Bake for 15-20 minutes, uncovered, or until the apples are fork-tender and the mixture thickens. Stir once or twice while it bakes.

# Lunch

## Vegetable Buckwheat Noodle Lunch

Prep Time: 5 minutes

Cook Time: 10-15 minutes

Serves: 1

**Ingredients:**

2 oz or 1¼ cup whole wheat noodle such as organic soba noodles, cooked

¾ cup of broccolini stems, cut along the length

¾ cup bok choy or green cabbage, ribboned

2 tsp toasted sesame oil

2 cups mushroom, vegetable or chicken broth

½ tsp Chinese 5-spice

2 small French breakfast or globe radishes, sliced in coin- shapes

1 small jalapeno (seeded and sliced into coins)

**Directions:**

1. Cook noodles a minute less than directed on the package, drain and toss with a teaspoon of sesame oil so it doesn't stick.

2. Steam cabbage and broccolini 1 minute.

3. Next, heat a skillet over a medium-high and then add the 1 teaspoon of sesame oil that's left. Add the cabbage and broccolini, sautéing 5 minutes or until just a bit charred. Remove and set aside.

4. Bring the broth to a boil, add the 5 spice and noodles, stirring well; remove.

5. Pour the broth, noodles, and veggies into a bowl. Add chilled radish and jalapeno to top. *Enjoy!*

# Dinner

## Whole-Wheat Spaghetti With Salmon, Lemon And Basil

*A healthy meal with protein and omega-3 rich salmon.*

Preparation time: 10 minutes

Cooking time: 10 minutes

Servings: 4

**Ingredients:**

1/2 lb whole grain or whole wheat spaghetti

2 tbsp extra-virgin olive oil

1 clove garlic, minced

1/2 tsp salt, + more for seasoning

1/2 tsp freshly ground black pepper, + more for seasoning

1 tbsp olive oil

4 (4-oz) pieces wild caught, Alaskan salmon

1/4 cup fresh basil leaves, chopped

3 tbsp capers

1 lemon, zested

2 tbsp lemon juice

2 cups fresh baby spinach leaves

**Directions:**

1. Cook pasta 8-10 minutes until al dente; drain and toss in a large bowl along with the extra-virgin olive oil, garlic, salt & pepper. Set aside.

2. In a medium skillet over medium-high temperature, warm the olive oil.

3. Now season the salmon with some salt and pepper and add to the skillet and cook until about 2 minutes per side or to your desire likeness. Remove fish from pan.

4. Add the capers, basil, lemon juice and lemon zest to the spaghetti mixture and toss well to combine.

5. Place 1/2 cup of spinach each in 4 bowls. Top with 1/4 pasta and then top with salmon. Enjoy!

## Snacks

Any of the snack ideas

*Chia Seeds*

**END**

Thank you for reading my book. If you enjoyed it, won't you please take a moment to leave me a review at your favorite retailer?

Thanks!

Matt Pyne